Breath, Death and Koheleth

A New, Secular Reading of Ecclesiastes

Chris Highland

© 2021 Chris Highland

Cover photograph by Chris Highland

Friendly Freethinker (www.chighland.com)

"In reality, not only the black letters but the white gaps in between, are symbols of the teaching, only that we are not able to read those gaps."

~Rabbi Levi Yitzhak *(in Tales of the Hasidim, Martin Buber)*

CONTENTS

INTRODUCTION

Squeezed in between the last chapter of Proverbs that ends with instructions for a good and capable wife, and the erotic love ballad, Song of Solomon, we find Ecclesiastes (in Hebrew: *Koheleth*: "the Preacher" or "The Teacher"). As far as I recall from biblical studies, no one really knows beyond doubt who wrote any of the ancient scriptures, Hebrew or Greek. That these specific three "books"—Proverbs, Ecclesiastes and Song of Solomon—are attributed to Solomon, son of King David of Israel (who lived about 3000 years ago), offers a hint of their origin, yet, as with most books of the Bible, scholars, like theologians, are at best "best guessers."

Eighteen pages, give or take. That's how many pages Koheleth takes in the Hebrew Bible. About eight pages in English (NRSV). That's with footnotes, so the point is there isn't much space for this teacher to teach or preacher to preach. He delivers his message, whatever that is, and hurries along to more pressing duties (presumably including visits with his 1000 politically-strategic "wives"). If the author was indeed the same king who arranged those "marriages" and utilized slave labor to build a temple in Jerusalem for his Lord, we have a clearer context for the troubled mind of the ruler who was "wiser than anyone else" on the planet (First Kings, 4).

Interesting to note, in the Hebrew Bible, where the

order of books is different than English, Song of Solomon/Song of Songs comes *before* Ecclesiastes and Lamentations *follows*. Ecclesiastes/Koheleth is near the end of sacred Jewish scriptures, considered among the Writings, following the Prophets which follow the Torah or first five books. Clear as Egyptian mud?

It has been said Ecclesiastes is "one of the deepest and most controversial books" and "contains some of the finest prose" in the Hebrew Bible. The book is often read in synagogues during Sukkot, the festival of tabernacles. When I was an Evangelical Pentecostal Campus Crusader, we really didn't know what to do with this puzzling book. It was better left hidden in the dark corners of the Bible (after all, the "New" Testament was far superior to the "Old"). A few passages were acceptable to recite from this confounding book, but Jesus never quoted from it, and you can't make catchy youthgroup songs from it! Later, as a minister, the question remained: How to preach The Preacher, or teach The Teacher?

As late rabbi Jonathan Sacks taught: "The book has seemed to many to be obscure, even self-contradictory. At times Kohelet seems miserable, at others, joyous. He is capable of hating life and loving life. His prose reads like a jumble of non-sequiturs. It's hard to say what the work as a whole is saying" ("Happiness is to be found in being, not in having," rabbisacks.org, October 25, 2008). Another rabbi bluntly states: "So many aspects of the book stand out to the reader as dismissive and sarcastic attacks on ways of life, not as a thoughtful philosophical reflection. Moreover, it is highly unusual for wisdom literature to dismiss the value of wisdom" (Prof. Rabbi Tzvee Zahavy, "Kohelet: An Israelite Form of Meditation," thetorah.com).

This brief study isn't really a study at all and certainly not scholarly. I am simply offering short reflections on the text itself (in the *New Revised Standard Version*) from the standpoint of *one freethinking secular humanist*. If it would help to define those terms, probably the best I can do at the present time, is this: a *secular* worldview is just that—a view of the world as the only world there is (perhaps Ecclesiastes affirms that?); *humanist* refers to an ethical way of life centered on human values, that human beings are responsible for our own actions in this secular world (Ecclesiastes?); and *freethinking* takes its cue from the non-traditional Freethought tradition that draws energy from reason and holds high the torch of liberty in conscience and community (a possible framework for understanding Ecclesiastes?).

A legitimate question might be: Why would a secular person, a former minister who left the ministry and is now a non-theist, continue to dig around in biblical soil? (A similar question could be posed about the columns I write for the religion pages of a local newspaper). Thanks for asking. Religion is clearly embedded in the psyche of human cultures and religious faith was integral to my being for many years. In fact, my journey through Protestant, Evangelical, Pentecostal, Ecumenical and Interfaith landscapes, reveals nearly a lifelong "dance" with the diverse drama of religion. Though this led to my eventual exit (exodus) from faith, I never lost the meaning of relationships—what I consider the core of faith communities anyway—and I stay connected to people of faith in family, friends and colleagues I care about and respect.

Significantly, the abiding depth of those relationships often originates in common experiences, working together—having similar commitments to serving others either motivated by faith or a compassionate humanism. I often refer to this *relation-foundation* in terms of **Co-words or Com-words**: Cooperation, Collaboration, Communication, naturally adding Compassion and Community. Religion at its best is all about the "Co" and that keeps me Co-nnected! Clearly, when religious practice forgets the "Co" it becomes destructive and dangerous (witness Christian Nationalism, or more directly related to our text here, *Biblicism*, when a book has more value than people). Here again, to some degree, I find the philosophical preacher named Koheleth an occasional Com-panion in the pursuit and practice of freethinking humanism.

As the Jewish Publication Society explains: "The Book of Ecclesiastes is part of the 'wisdom literature' of the Bible. It concerns itself with universal philosophical questions, rather than events in the history of Israel and in the Hebrews' covenant with God. Koheleth, the speaker in this book, ruminates on what—if anything—has lasting value, and how—if at all—God interacts with humankind. Koheleth expresses bewilderment and frustration at life's absurdities and injustices. He grapples with the inequities that pervade the world and the frailty and limitations of human wisdom and right-eousness. His awareness of these discomfiting facts coexists with a firm belief in God's rule and God's funda-mental justice, and he looks for ways to define a mean-ingful life in a world where so much is senseless."

Secular ears will pick up on the phrase: "how—*if at all* —God interacts." What's God up to, what kind of God are we talking about, and does this God even exist? This could cause heartburn for some believers, yet even in my evangelical college, sitting in an "Old Testament" class, we grappled with similar disturbances raised by various biblical texts. Ironically, I suppose, my faith seemed to weather the storms of skepticism and I gained a more balanced respect for the context and con-undrums contained in scriptures. In seminary, espe-cially while studying Latin American, Native American, Feminist and Black "Liberation Theologians," the con-textual disturbance took a central position in anything concerning faith. This was an early wake-up for me. Ministry should be service and that ought to be outside the walls of the Church; further, the Bible couldn't be central when people should be.

As originally written, the Hebrew Bible had no verses or even punctuation and the wonderful challenges of the language and literature resolve into clearer focus ... or foggy blur! That out-of-focus sense leads the reader to acknowledge consistent uncertainties (as well as incon-sistencies) while holding up various lenses in the quest for clarity—a clearer picture of the instructive narrative —at the same time the reader is scanning for other ways of reading, alternate interpretations.

In this book, from a secular perspective, we will explore passages and pericopes to present interpretations aside from or beyond the theological. First and foremost, Ecclesiastes/Koheleth is Hebrew literature and therefore Jewish scripture. I will respect that context throughout. However, my concern is to draw out wisdom, or call out nonsense (if and when I see it), in order to offer a message or multiple messages that a person of another faith or other secular people could appreciate. I'm not out to convince anyone of anything, to convert anyone to a humanist outlook. Yet, I am attempting to wrestle with the text (in good traditional rabbinic style) to see if there are relevant words, concepts, ideas, stories, that may apply to our own time, believer or not.

Of my other little book of biblical reflections, *The Message on the Mountain: A New Secular Reading of The Sermon on the Mount*, a retired Christian educator wrote that he used the book in a "spiritual retreat" with a group of friends. He said: "It went very well and our friends are now searching for more of your writings and musings. Thank you for being the writer, thinker, and philosopher we can use as a mentor and guide to seeking a better path." This delightful response energized me to continue my infrequent visits to the old book I still carry in my mental backpack after all these years. The Bible used to be the only book I really needed to guide my life, then joined other "holy books" as a source of wisdom, ultimately joining them alongside books of Nature, Science, Philosophy, History, Poetry, Social Justice and more on my bookshelves.

Regarding collected wisdom literature, to the extent the Bible itself is a compendium of diverse books, I suppose I chose Ecclesiastes in the Hebrew scriptures for the same reason I chose the so-called Sermon on the Mount in the Christian scriptures. They both epitomize poetic preaching with a secular flair. Both these selections are, on some level, my defaults when it comes to fundamentally relevant ethical teachings. As I say of the "Sermon," you can pretty much toss out the rest of the "New Testament." I could be wrong, but in my view, it could be argued Koheleth assumes that position in the older literature. Not that we should eliminate the story of Israel as the history of a people, but the philosophical heart of the story may beat in the pages of Koheleth. To be sure, that's a tenuous and tentative assumption.

This is obviously not an extensive analysis of Ecclesiastes. Needless to say, I'm only scratching the surface of the holy scroll, yet I hope to at least put my finger on any remaining pulse to see if anything remains alive in these pages. Who knows if some of us, especially those who no longer see a divine finger at work in these ancient words, can perhaps present a fresh, vibrant, relevant reading for our uncertain time. Does Koheleth hold crucial keys and questions for our day?

If *Breath, Death and Koheleth* lends itself to personal reflection, group discussion or even preaching with The

Preacher, it might deserve a space on any bookshelf.

Chris Highland
Asheville, North Carolina
Autumn, 2021

To Teachers
of the
Questions

CHAPTER ONE
Life Is But A Breath

Chapter 1: 1-11

1 The words of the Teacher, the son of David, king in Jerusalem.

2 Vanity of vanities, says the Teacher, vanity of vanities! All is vanity.

3 What do people gain from all the toil at which they toil under the sun?

4 A generation goes, and a generation comes, but the earth remains forever.

5 The sun rises and the sun goes down, and hurries to the place where it rises.

6 The wind blows to the south, and goes around to the north; round and round goes the wind, and on its circuits the wind returns.

7 All streams run to the sea, but the sea is not full; to the place where the streams flow, there they continue to flow.

8 All things are wearisome; more than one can express; the eye is not satisfied with seeing, or the ear filled with hearing.

9 What has been is what will be, and what has been done is what will be done; there is nothing new under the sun.

10 Is there a thing of which it is said, "See, this is new"? It has already been, in the ages before us.

11 The people of long ago are not remembered, nor will

there be any remembrance of people yet to come by those who come after them.

COMMENTS

anity: from Latin *vanitas*, *vanus*: "empty." Worthless, futile, empty. Interesting to note another definition: "excessive pride or admiration of one's own appearance or achievements." Koheleth the Teacher seems to be wrestling with both meanings. His lecture, if we can call it that, is about looking closely, uncomfortably in the mirror, then out the windows at the wider world. Mirrors and windows. We might keep these glass portals in mind. This is about seeing deeper and higher, with both narrow and wider vision. A computer screen dark, empty, reflective, or bright, clear and full of possibilities.

Emerson's friend and colleague, writer Margaret Fuller, beautifully expressed this sentiment: "I cannot live without my own particular star; but my foot is on the earth and I wish to walk over it until my wings be grown. I will use my microscope as well as my telescope" (letter to her friend Caroline, May 1837). Mirror, window; microscope, telescope, screen. All useful when fearlessly facing the uselessness.

This bonfire of the vanities has burned for a very long time. The writer stares into the flames and proclaims it's all vanity, all worthless, meaningless, and he feels helpless and hopeless (a helpless King! woe to the subjects!). What's the use? What good is all this stuff we do? And this is only the Professor's opening statement. Imagine how readers might immediately respond, does this feel inviting to readers or turning them off from reading any further? We can judge that for ourselves as we proceed.

We might keep an eye on all the natural images he uses here and throughout. He's observant, a kind of naturalistic philosopher, noticing the order and flow of things. The sun, wind, streams, sea. While observing a high mountain environment, naturalist John Muir wrote: "Contemplating the lace-like fabric of streams outspread over the mountains, we are reminded that everything is flowing" (*My First Summer in the Sierra*). The mountaineer points with delight to the incessant movement of the waters, the winds, animals, birds, snows, even rocks and stars! It's that flow, and that "fabric," that The Teacher is aware of. Yet, that awareness is painful for him as it never was for Muir.

The pessimism of these opening verses take us down into the dark valleys (shadow of death?) and presents our first graphic description of the author's sense of futility and vulnerability. You almost imagine him on stage with Mick Jagger belting out: "I Can't Get No Satisfaction!" Then he collapses on stage gasping for breath: "All things are wearisome ... there is no satisfaction ... all is ultimately worthless ... nothing matters" and cries out: "It's all been done and seen and heard before. Let me out of here!"

Maybe there's nothing much new under the sun or moon or stars. Yet, it's all new, isn't it, every moment of every new day? Mick Jagger meets George Harrison:

"Here Comes the Sun!" An exclamation of life's worth and the value of every "little darling" (child or spouse) who lives each fresh day.

But Koheleth isn't there. Yet. And maybe he'll never make it. We'll see.

CHAPTER 1: 12-18

12 I, the Teacher, when king over Israel in Jerusalem,
13 applied my mind to seek and to search out by wisdom all that is done under heaven; it is an unhappy business that God has given to human beings to be busy with.
14 I saw all the deeds that are done under the sun; and see, all is vanity and a chasing after wind.
15 What is crooked cannot be made straight, and what is lacking cannot be counted.
16 I said to myself, "I have acquired great wisdom, surpassing all who were over Jerusalem before me; and my mind has had great experience of wisdom and knowledge."
17 And I applied my mind to know wisdom and to know madness and folly. I perceived that this also is but a chasing after wind.
18 For in much wisdom is much vexation, and those who increase knowledge increase sorrow.

COMMENTS

Accumulating knowledge enhanced by wisdom is tricky for students as well as teachers. Acquiring a "good" balanced education requires courage and determination even in the face of danger (compare how some Islamic states treat education, especially for girls, and the distrust of public education by many Christianists). For freethinkers who push beyond the restrictions of orthodoxy in both classroom and cathedral, even asking incisive questions in the search for truth and wisdom can walk us straight into paradox. As James Baldwin stated to teachers:

"The paradox of education is precisely this–that as one begins to become conscious one begins to examine the society in which he is being educated. The purpose of education, finally, is to create in a person the ability to look at the world for himself, to make his own decisions, to say to himself this is black or this is white, to decide for himself whether there is a God in heaven or not. To ask questions of the universe, and then learn to live with those questions, is the way he achieves his own identity. But no society is really anxious to have that kind of person around. What societies really, ideally, want is a citizenry which will simply obey the rules of society. If a society succeeds in this, that society is about to perish" ("A Talk to Teachers," *The Saturday Review*, December 21, 1963).

This may cause us to be curious how "The Teacher" was received in his own community or realm. We could guess they weren't anxious to have this educator around—he asked too many questions, unsettling questions, and seemed to encourage students to strive for that "ability to look at the world for [themselves]," to decide for themselves what was true and good and wise. In fact, as I see it, reading Baldwin (especially *The Fire Next Time*) alongside Koheleth would be an education in itself. A contemporary writer and social critic asking hard questions and challenging societal and religious norms, Baldwin potentially speaks to a number of the same disturbances in the human psyche and human community as The Teacher. The main caveat would be Baldwin, while possibly agreeing with much of The Professor's instruction, would at the same time call him to task for his treatment of women, ownership of slaves, and other political policies exacerbating the oppression of his own land. Precisely because James Baldwin emerged from early life as a preacher to critique the religio-political abuse of power, he, along with many of our contemporary social critics and reformers, might be just what Koheleth needed then, and his interpreters need now.

"Vexation" is a good word. Annoyance, irritation, exasperation—all appropriate terms for the smart but somber writer, who seems to be comprehending the common sense lesson spoken by one comic character: "The more I learn the smarter I get, the smarter I get the more I realize how much I have to learn." It can surely be exasperating to store a great deal of knowledge in the head only to consistently discover your knowledge is limited, that there is so much more to learn. Yet, as annoying as that can be, isn't this the unending task of education and the practice of wisdom? Vexing, indeed, but essential.

The Teacher walks face-first into the web of wisdom, stuck to the same strands that caught Lao Tzu in the Tao: "Look for it, it cannot be seen ... Listen for it, it cannot be heard ... Reach for it, it cannot be touched ... Go to meet it, you cannot see its face" (*Tao Te Ching*, 14).

This section introduces one of the most intriguing images in Koheleth: "chasing after wind." An elusive, if not comical, image. Translators suggest it could also be read as: "feeding on wind." We'll return to this along the way since wind/breath is a central theme in the book.

In fact, I suggest the reader substitute "Breath" for every reference to "God" in the text. In my view, our creator is Breath, a natural, this-world, secular gift at birth, returned at death--in our last breath.

NOTES & QUESTIONS

CHAPTER TWO
Eat, Drink, Find Joy

Chapter 2: 1-11

1 I said to myself, "Come now, I will make a test of pleasure; enjoy yourself." But again, this also was vanity.

2 I said of laughter, "It is mad," and of pleasure, "What use is it?"

3 I searched with my mind how to cheer my body with wine—my mind still guiding me with wisdom—and how to lay hold on folly, until I might see what was good for mortals to do under heaven during the few days of their life.

4 I made great works; I built houses and planted vineyards for myself;

5 I made myself gardens and parks, and planted in them all kinds of fruit trees.

6 I made myself pools from which to water the forest of growing trees.

7 I bought male and female slaves, and had slaves who were born in my house; I also had great possessions of herds and flocks, more than any who had been before me in Jerusalem.

8 I also gathered for myself silver and gold and the treasure of kings and of the provinces; I got singers, both men and women, and delights of the flesh, and many concubines.

9 So I became great and surpassed all who were before me in Jerusalem; also my wisdom remained with me.

10 Whatever my eyes desired I did not keep from them; I kept my heart from no pleasure, for my heart found pleasure in all my toil, and this was my reward for all my toil.

11 Then I considered all that my hands had done and the toil I had spent in doing it, and again, all was vanity and a chasing after wind, and there was nothing to be gained under the sun.

COMMENTS

Though the writer has major blindspots, radically honest self-reflection is a major thread running through the whole book. Many "I" statements reveal an attitude of deep introspection. "I said," "I searched," "I made," etc. And we begin to hear more intensity of self-doubt (and self-incrimination) as if the writer is arriving at a measure of admission: "I might be wrong" or "Did I miss something in Life's manual?" (which of course doesn't exist).

Is The Teacher advocating unbridled hedonism? In one sense, I think he is—but it makes a difference what "bridle" is used. For many believers, that would be "God is watching, and judging," while humanists might think "What impact does seeking after my own pleasure have on others?" Morality, or ethics. Throughout our text this is a golden thread—or wireless connection. How connected am I to others and what effect does my behavior have on their lives? However a person frames that, as a faith frame or freethought frame, the issue is the same: In what way is my "I" related to "We." A contemporary parallel might be the fractures in American society over "My rights (beliefs and privileges) are foremost" over against the democratic ideal of "We the People"—what's best for the most is what's truly best. Then we join the two century debate over who decides what is best and how that would be enforced ("encouraged" through legislation?).

"Anything you want, you got it," sang Roy Orbison. Koheleth sings in response: "I got it all, so now what?"

The poetry of The Teacher begins to come to the forefront here. And in those "I" statements those familiar with Walt Whitman may smile with recognition. This is a kind of ancient "Song of Myself." Whitman's identity with the encircling environment, absorbing the good, bad and ugly into himself, embodying nature both creative and destructive, seems related to the Teacher's obsession (if we can call it that) with interacting with the world he sees and his own pleasures and pains. As Whitman describes in his startling poem "This Compost": "Behold, this compost! behold it well! … What chemistry! … Now I am terrified at the Earth, it is that calm and patient. It grows such sweet things out of such corruptions. It turns harmless and stainless on its axis, with such endless successions of diseased corpses." He suddenly feels fear of catching something from the "compost" of the earth, before comprehending the chemical cleansing of the soil, and delighting in his own bodily compost.

The delight, the celebration, the participatory though transitory joy of Whitman is missing in The Teacher who seems greatly distracted by the contradictions within himself and in his world. He is a kingdom of one in a realm full of people and empty of meaning. Unlike Whitman, he cannot absorb the suffering. There is no sense he would be found reading poetry to wounded soldiers in Civil War hospitals.

What's the use of work? He finds no lasting meaning or purpose in his labor. We might counsel him, as the secular chaplain Whitman surely would: "It sounds like your work is all about *you*? Why not drop the royal robes and do something positive, constructive, truly healthy and helpful for others? Use your incredible position of power to *seek to serve, not be served*. Get your mind off yourself, man! There may be pleasures far greater than you imagine, and they don't depend on what you eat and drink."

This is the Teacher's disabling blindspot. Ironically, now he speaks of darkness, even while holding up the only lantern he knows.

12 So I turned to consider wisdom and madness and folly; for what can the one do who comes after the king? Only what has already been done.

13 Then I saw that wisdom excels folly as light excels darkness.

14 The wise have eyes in their head, but fools walk in darkness.

Yet I perceived that the same fate befalls all of them.

15 Then I said to myself, "What happens to the fool will happen to me also; why then have I been so very wise?" And I said to myself that this also is vanity.

16 For there is no enduring remembrance of the wise or of fools, seeing that in the days to come all will have been long forgotten. How can the wise die just like fools?

17 So I hated life, because what is done under the sun was grievous to me; for all is vanity and a chasing after wind.

18 I hated all my toil in which I had toiled under the sun, seeing that I must leave it to those who come after me

19 —and who knows whether they will be wise or foolish? Yet they will be master of all for which I toiled and used my wisdom under the sun. This also is vanity.

20 So I turned and gave my heart up to despair concerning all the toil of my labors under the sun,

21 because sometimes one who has toiled with wisdom and knowledge and skill must leave all to be enjoyed by another who did not toil for it. This also is vanity and a

great evil.

22 What do mortals get from all the toil and strain with which they toil under the sun?

23 For all their days are full of pain, and their work is a vexation; even at night their minds do not rest. This also is vanity.

24 There is nothing better for mortals than to eat and drink, and find enjoyment in their toil. This also, I saw, is from the hand of God;

25 for apart from him who can eat or who can have enjoyment?

26 For to the one who pleases him God gives wisdom and knowledge and joy; but to the sinner he gives the work of gathering and heaping, only to give to one who pleases God. This also is vanity and a chasing after wind.

COMMENTS

In praise of wisdom, the goddess Hochmah/Sophia (for reference see esp. Proverbs 8: "Does not wisdom call? ... The Creator created me at the beginning of his work, the first of his acts of long ago ... I was beside him like a master worker, and I was daily his delight,"). Yet, what is Her masterwork now? Where will She take you? Where does wisdom get you? Who knows if you will be foolish or wise, and what does it matter anyway? *Already deep in his lecture, he's still trying to catch his breath, feed on the wind, find sanity in the vanity.* Can he? Does he succeed? The light and delight of wisdom and reason lights the way, but it remains elusive, maddeningly out of reach.

In *Dust Tracks on a Road*, Zora Neale Hurston writes: "Grown people know that they do not always know the why of things, and even if they think they know, they do not know where and how they got the proof." The wind is picking up, the dust is blowing.

"The wise have eyes in their head," yet our Teacher seems to feel like the person in the Beatles' song, "The Fool on the Hill": "But the fool on the hill; Sees the sun going down; And the eyes in his head; See the world spinning round." Instead of appreciating those powers of observation, he gets stuck spinning in comparisons of the wise and the fools. This takes him down the rabbit hole of hating life and climbing foolishly up a hill convinced work has no reward.

Here we see the writer's *faith in full display*, and it isn't pretty to see. If there *is* any enjoyment, fulfillment, happiness, it comes "from the hand of God." This capricious deity may reward a person with pleasure (or feed them breath) or not. And how does one "please" this pleasure- or pain-giving God? So far in our reading, The Teacher has nothing to preach about that. It all seems vain, empty and senseless. Even the sensual pleasures are senseless. Why? He has no idea except if you gain some wisdom you may become more aware of the futility of gaining that wisdom. It's almost like a person who hikes to the summit of a mountain only to look down and see it's all a wrecked and wretched world below. Another example may be the native chief who listens to the fire and brimstone sermon of the missionary in his village, responding: "Why did you tell us about hell? Now that we know, we're damned!"

Koheleth wrestles with the contradictions that tear him in two. Even when he tries to be happy he feels the emptiness: "I gave my heart up to despair."

One of the greatest orators in American history was the "Great Agnostic," Robert Green Ingersoll who once said: "Happiness Is the Only Good, Reason the Only Torch, Justice the Only Worship, Humanity the Only Religion and Love the Only Priest" (*Collected Works*, motto opening Vol. 8).

Another tidbit of wisdom from Ingersoll could have helped usher The Teacher through his "dark night of the soul." Ingersoll flatly stated: "He who enslaves another cannot be free" ("Decoration Day Oration"). Koheleth's internal suffering may well be traced time and again to his ownership of other human beings. Slaveowners and abusers of women will never find wisdom or be free or happy.

Ingersoll's personal "creed" would have pleased Koheleth, at least on a good day: "Happiness is the only good. The place to be happy is here. The time to be happy is now. The way to be happy is to make others so" ("The Tendency of Modern Thought"). We might note once more that The Teacher appeared to have the hardest time with the last part of Ingersoll's creed—to make others happy comes first and will bring you happiness.

With his incessant attitude of platitudes, he finds instead of happiness, hate. "So I hated life, because what is done under the sun was grievous to me; for all is vanity and a chasing after wind." More and more it becomes clear: this Teacher needs some fresh air, a higher perspective than he gets from the confines of his castle or the tower in the temple. He's already acknowledged that he notices the flow of things beneath the sun, around the sun. But he needs another perch, another voice, a naturalist's perspective.

In 1915, popular writer and nature essayist John Burroughs, published *The Breath of Life*. Emerging from his own religious family life, Burroughs became a strong proponent of the natural world as good and beautiful enough, without any supernatural. For him, God and Nature were identical—with a keen eye and curiosity he studied his environment as the only classroom and cathedral necessary. After writing *The Light of Day* (1900) and before writing his last book, *Accepting the Universe* (1921), Burroughs wrote, among other works, *The Breath of Life* where he said: *"There is tremendous activity in the air we breathe, in the water we drink, in the food we eat, and in the soil we walk upon, which, if magnified till our senses could take it in, would probably drive us mad."* Physicists, biologists and an array of who we may call "natural clergy," guide us in our search to understand our world. What would Koheleth think, what would he do, what would he say, if he could look through a microscope or telescope to expand his universe? Wouldn't he think it wonderful, as we do, and "get out of himself" for a while?

John Burroughs closes *The Breath of Life* with a chapter entitled, "The Naturalist's View of Life," and we could imagine, or wish, that our Teacher had read this before, or after, writing his lecture. Burroughs feeds us our breath, places us where we belong, in the whole circle of life: *"Brooded by the sun, the earth hatched her offspring ... All that we call the spiritual, the divine, the celestial, are the earth's, because we are hers. Our religions and our philosophies and our literatures are hers: humanity is a part of the whole system of things; we are not an alien, nor an accident ... we are here as the rains, the dews, the flowers, the rocks, the soil, the trees, are here ... . We are of the same stuff as the ground we walk upon."* Then he speaks as if directly to The Teacher: *"We cannot magnify humanity without magnifying the universe of which we are a part; and we cannot belittle it without belittling ourselves"* (I've used inclusive language in the quotation). Indeed, he concludes: "Science has made us at home in the universe."

For Burroughs, and many freethinking minds like his, nature is truly enough. And the fact that everything is in constant flow and change means, for our modern scientific mindset, all things *are* new, day by day, moment by moment, under the sun, moon, stars and galaxies.

Though at times we feel the stranger, we are truly at home. As Martin Luther King, Jr. expressed it: "We have inherited a large house, a great 'world-house' in which we have to live together" (*Where Do We Go From Here?*). There's a strong wind blowing through the house.

NOTES & QUESTIONS

CHAPTER THREE
What Goes Around, Comes Around

Chapter 3: 1-8

1 For everything there is a season, and a time for every matter under heaven:

2 a time to be born, and a time to die; a time to plant, and a time to pluck up what is planted;

3 a time to kill, and a time to heal; a time to break down, and a time to build up;

4 a time to weep, and a time to laugh; a time to mourn, and a time to dance;

5 a time to throw away stones, and a time to gather stones together; a time to embrace, and a time to refrain from embracing;

6 a time to seek, and a time to lose; a time to keep, and a time to throw away;

7 a time to tear, and a time to sew; a time to keep silence, and a time to speak;

8 a time to love, and a time to hate; a time for war, and a time for peace.

COMMENTS

IF it's possible to unplug the Byrd's song, "Turn, Turn, Turn" from our brain speakers for a minute, we may "turn up" a much deeper lesson here. Is this famous poetic passage really about seasons of experience, comparing this and that? As another song of the 70's lyrically said: "Does Anybody Really Know What Time it Is?" (Chicago).

There's a time for everything, but there's no watch big enough to tell us what time it is, now, now, now. Moment by moment, day by day, life by life, the seasons pass. All we can do is take a deep breath, then another, and take the seasons as they come. He guesses. Isn't that all we can do, guess?

Yet, The Teacher is caught in a time-warp, with no watch, but he hears an alarm clock and can't turn it off. Why is it ringing? What can I do? It's his "time to speak" but maybe it's really the "time to keep silence." How can he know?

Can anyone honestly say: "Oh, we're just in a time of war, not peace," or, "Now is just the time, the season, to kill, or hate"? At their worst, these eight verses lend themselves to the awful, tone-deafness when someone says to a loved one who's suffering or dying, "It's your time to suffer, to die," or "It's your season to weep and mourn." We know scriptures are often used in this terrible way, yet Koheleth passes that into their hands. Is there another way to take this?

During my "seminary of the streets," the years following formal graduate training, I learned an incredible amount from jail inmates and streetpeople. One thing I heard in jail was the common refrain: "What goes around, comes around." This fit in neatly with the description of the jail itself as a "revolving door." People entered and exited, came and went, over and over again. As a chaplain I frequently exclaimed: "You're back! Why are you back in here again?" A detained person might respond: "I'm S.O.S. (stuck on stupid), trapped in the cycle of bad decisions, drugs, detention." Something like that. I'm not sure how helpful Koheleth would be for them, for that chaplaincy. A person commits a murder, would he say, "There's a time to kill"? A person is homeless, would he respond: "There's a time to lose"?

Perhaps there comes a "time" to stop trying to make sense of the world by pairing everything! Maybe this is not the season for "seasons," for merely packaging the events of life in neat boxes, to say: "Well, it's just *The Time*."

In *The Varieties of Scientific Experience*, Carl Sagan wrote: *"I think if we ever reach the point where we think we thoroughly understand who we are and where we came from, we will have failed. [The search for answers] goes with a courageous intent to greet the universe as it really is ... to courageously accept what our explorations tell us."* For Koheleth, and perhaps for us, "the time has come"-- it's the season for courage.

9 What gain have the workers from their toil?

10 I have seen the business that God has given to everyone to be busy with.

11 He has made everything suitable for its time; moreover he has put a sense of past and future into their minds, yet they cannot find out what God has done from the beginning to the end.

12 I know that there is nothing better for them than to be happy and enjoy themselves as long as they live;

13 moreover, it is God's gift that all should eat and drink and take pleasure in all their toil.

14 I know that whatever God does endures forever; nothing can be added to it, nor anything taken from it; God has done this, so that all should stand in awe before him.

15 That which is, already has been; that which is to be, already is; and God seeks out what has gone by.

16 Moreover I saw under the sun that in the place of justice, wickedness was there, and in the place of righteousness, wickedness was there as well.

17 I said in my heart, God will judge the righteous and the wicked, for he has appointed a time for every matter, and for every work.

18 I said in my heart with regard to human beings that God is testing them to show that they are but animals.

19 For the fate of humans and the fate of animals is the same; as one dies, so dies the other. They all have the same breath, and humans have no advantage over the

animals; for all is vanity.

20 All go to one place; all are from the dust, and all turn to dust again.

21 Who knows whether the human spirit goes upward and the spirit of animals goes downward to the earth?

22 So I saw that there is nothing better than that all should enjoy their work, for that is their lot; who can bring them to see what will be after them?

COMMENTS

The CEO in their highrise office looks down on the ants below. Maybe s/he feels the view is similar to God looking down on humanity? What is the Chief Executive watching for? Why does s/he give different work to different people? What's the pay, the salary, what are the benefits?

People have "a sense of past and future" but can never seem to comprehend what the heck God is up to—what it's all about. Exasperating, isn't it? The Boss does things and we don't know why. There are no explanations just vexations. The writer's faith rests (uneasily) on the tenuous assurance that God gives, God takes away, and what's the purpose? "So that all should stand in awe before him."

There's no nice way to say it: This God appears to be playing with people, moving us around the proverbial chess board to win one thing: our praise, admiration, worship. This is Ego (or Selfishness) deified. The Teacher is on the edge of resignation. It's no use resisting; leave it all in the Boss's hands. The factory whistle sounds like an alarm, the refrain echoes: "Sixteen tons, what do you get, another day older and deeper in debt ... I owe my soul to the Company store."

"I said in my heart." He is bothered that where there is justice there is injustice, when there is something right, there is something not right close at hand. Well, he seems to say to himself, God will sort it all out later. Or maybe God is testing us, reminding us we're not much different than other animals. After all, we share the same breath, feed on the wind on the same earth. "Dust to dust," and breath to breath—it's really all the same: worthless, meaningless. We can't know what comes after our dust and breath dissipates like other creatures. So what? What now? Do whatever work you can find, do what you enjoy, and that's it.

"All go to one place." Some imagine heaven, others Eden. Or, we might wonder if Lakota elder Black Elk, in one of his final prayers to the "Grandfather, the Great Spirit," truly honored the old dust of earth when he cried out: *"To the center of the world you have taken me and showed the goodness and the beauty and the strangeness of the greening earth, the only mother ... at the center of this sacred hoop you have said that I should make the tree to bloom"* (*Black Elk Speaks*). He felt he had been given "a sacred wind" and all powers of the earth would aid his watering the deep-rooted tree of his tribe, and humanity itself.

Like Koheleth, Black Elk felt despair at what he saw, but he never lost sight of the tree rising from the dust of which we're made.

NOTES & QUESTIONS

CHAPTER FOUR
Pressed, Oppressed Or Depressed

Chapter 4: 1-8

1 Again I saw all the oppressions that are practiced under the sun. Look, the tears of the oppressed—with no one to comfort them! On the side of their oppressors there was power—with no one to comfort them.

2 And I thought the dead, who have already died, more fortunate than the living, who are still alive;

3 but better than both is the one who has not yet been, and has not seen the evil deeds that are done under the sun.

4 Then I saw that all toil and all skill in work come from one person's envy of another. This also is vanity and a chasing after wind.

5 Fools fold their hands and consume their own flesh.

6 Better is a handful with quiet than two handfuls with toil, and a chasing after wind.

7 Again, I saw vanity under the sun:

8 the case of solitary individuals, without sons or brothers; yet there is no end to all their toil, and their eyes are never satisfied with riches. "For whom am I toiling," they ask, "and depriving myself of pleasure?" This also is vanity and an unhappy business.

COMMENTS

A rather fascinating viewpoint presented here. Thankfully, he not only observes oppressed people but sees their tears; he shows sympathy for the fact that no one is comforting them. But as we know, there are "good people on both sides" (I'm being sarcastic here). Powerful oppressors have no comforters either. He doesn't see any tears in their eyes. Well, where will our teacher take this?

So, if you're dead, you're fortunate. Even better if you were never born!

This should not be read by someone entering college or a trade school. He's blowing off a lot of steam here, but it's chilling. He looks around and sees vanity everywhere, with everyone. Work and gain a little, or work and gain a fortune, it's all hot air and it smells bad too.

An important lesson not to miss. A central question millions ask day by day: "For whom am I working?" How many work hard and have so little at the end of the day? How many sit back in their plush offices, resting on their inherited wealth, and the stocks keep paying off? Is any of it fair, or just, or "God's will"? The wake-up call comes when a person anywhere on the economic ladder realizes it's "an unhappy business."

Who is satisfied with what they make, what they have, who they are? Maybe they're lucky if they are satisfied, but are they content? Contentment can't be earned and doesn't come with increase in possessions or power. At least Koheleth hints at a first step toward inner and interpersonal contentment: have some empathy for the tears of others.

Emerson awoke from a dream and picked up his journal: "After some more sleepings and wakings I shall lie on this mattress sick; then, dead; and through [my doorway] they will carry these bones. Where shall I be then?" He concludes, "I lifted my head and beheld the spotless orange light of the morning beaming up from the dark hills into the wide Universe" (October, 1837). The thought of death and dying doesn't have to be oppressive when we look beyond our own doorways to see ourselves in the natural light of day.

As for those who face failure in their efforts to respond to oppression and injustice, the experience of early American activists is instructive: *"These activists knew their aims were utopian and had every reason to expect defeat, but they tried for them anyway. All that they accomplished was fired by this mix of radical hope and unrelenting antagonism, their willingness to hazard failure rather than accept the world as they found it"* (Holly Jackson, *American Radicals*).

In facing and fearing his own failures and the failures all around him, was Koheleth resigned to defeat? In resisting any potential fire of radical hope did he neglect to take an alternative action, to say to himself and his student-readers: "This world can be unjust, unfair, unfathomable, but we, I, cannot accept that the world must always be this way."

CHAPTER 4: 9-16

9 Two are better than one, because they have a good reward for their toil.

10 For if they fall, one will lift up the other; but woe to one who is alone and falls and does not have another to help.

11 Again, if two lie together, they keep warm; but how can one keep warm alone?

12 And though one might prevail against another, two will withstand one. A threefold cord is not quickly broken.

13 Better is a poor but wise youth than an old but foolish king, who will no longer take advice.

14 One can indeed come out of prison to reign, even though born poor in the kingdom.

15 I saw all the living who, moving about under the sun, follow that youth who replaced the king;

16 there was no end to all those people whom he led. Yet those who come later will not rejoice in him. Surely this also is vanity and a chasing after wind.

COMMENTS

Is the Preaching Professor finally suggesting a solution, or positive response to our useless toil, our shortness of breath? Cooperative work has its rewards. There can be practice results from striving, standing or even sleeping with another person. Here, he's taking a constructive step outside himself, considering the benefits of friends, companions, partners. Did he feel that with any of his wives?

You may be young and poor, but if you live by wisdom you're actually in a better position than an older person with power and possessions.

While preparing for chaplaincy I read the book, *The Rich Get Richer and the Poor Get Prison*, that described the hard-to-hear truth about the American prison industry. For many, especially poor people of color, justice can seem like a cruel joke, a dream long in coming, if it ever arrives. Koheleth/Solomon may have had his father King David of Israel in mind, as a young man who defeated King Saul. Though David didn't come out of prison, he became a fugitive running from Saul's crazed anger. Whether or not Koheleth was referring to his father, the legendary parable presents the potential for even the most unlikely person to rise to higher position. And yet ... true to form ... The Teacher can't let that heroic story stand as a real possibility for balancing inequality and injustice. History won't be kind to the young hero, so it's worthless. He'll be forgotten, and so will his son. It's time to take a deep and disappointing breath again. He's left in emptiness, again.

Is he in a self-imposed prison in his own mind?

In *The People, Yes*, Carl Sandburg offers The Teacher, and his students, a more expansive vision: "The stars make no noise. You can't hinder the wind from blowing. Who could live without hope?" (94).

No, Koheleth, you can't hinder the wind from blowing, and hope may be all you have. Who will remember the youth, the king, anyone? Ironically, here, in these pages, we are reading the woeful, breathless refrain of The Teacher, all these centuries later. We remember.

NOTES & QUESTIONS

CHAPTER FIVE
Can't Take It With You

Chapter 5: 1-7

1 Guard your steps when you go to the house of God; to draw near to listen is better than the sacrifice offered by fools; for they do not know how to keep from doing evil.
2 Never be rash with your mouth, nor let your heart be quick to utter a word before God, for God is in heaven, and you upon earth; therefore let your words be few.
3 For dreams come with many cares, and a fool's voice with many words.
4 When you make a vow to God, do not delay fulfilling it; for he has no pleasure in fools. Fulfill what you vow.
5 It is better that you should not vow than that you should vow and not fulfill it.
6 Do not let your mouth lead you into sin, and do not say before the messenger that it was a mistake; why should God be angry at your words, and destroy the work of your hands?
7 With many dreams come vanities and a multitude of words; but fear God.

COMMENTS

Elohim (The God or gods) plays a larger role in this chapter, and it's a very odd role. As in chapter 3, this maddeningly elusive divinity is both Giver and Taker. If it's accurate to say the name *Elohim* refers to a plurality of gods (as in the Genesis creation story), maybe it wouldn't be too much of a stretch to conjecture The King/Teacher here senses he shares a kind of divine schizophrenia. Elohim creates heaven and earth, male and female, and demands obedience, testing that by planting a Tree of Knowledge in the middle of the Garden. In a sense, The Teacher faces the same choice. He chooses knowledge and loses paradise. The greatest act of humanity, to choose, is also our downfall, at least in one narrative. Any faith he holds onto is a faith where choice may not immediately or ultimately matter because everything he perceives and chooses is a breath of dust, empty words, reaching for the unreachable. He's eaten of the Tree of Knowledge and is left with taking a deep breath of earth-flavored dust.

You can go to the House of God, the temple in Jerusalem, built by Solomon, but keep in mind the prayer he spoke at the dedication: "But will God really dwell on earth? The heavens, even the highest heaven, cannot contain you. How much less this temple I have built!" (First Kings 8). The Fool on the Hill. He builds a house for the Creator of the Universe. No surprise—it's not big enough! The gods are in heaven, we're on earth, so watch your mouth, take care what you say. The mouth, words, vows, all these matter because the gods might be angry with what you say when you rattle off many words … so, be afraid, be very afraid.

This seems to be instruction about prayer and making promises. We should watch our tongue and listen more than speak because God is listening and could destroy all the vain work God has given us to do.

The deity or deities presented here would encourage a King to build a temple (using extreme wealth, resources and slave labor) no god would ever fit inside, and then require few words so as not to make the deity/ies angry since he/they might come down hard on the people and their work.

The impression or image we're left with: a temple with a huge banner hanging over the doorway—"Warning, watch what you say here!" Or, as the prophet Habakkuk instructs those entering the temple: "Let all the earth keep silence before [Breath]." For, as he says, an idol "has no breath in it" (2:19-20).

Rabbi Abraham Joshua Heschel said: "Man is a messenger who forgot the message." And perhaps religion tends to forget who humankind is, making the "image of god" central without respecting the other side of creation's coin. As Heschel reminds biblical readers: "[Human beings have been] formed out of the dust of the earth" (*I Asked for Wonder*). Why fear the god created in our own image?

CHAPTER 5: 8-20

8 If you see in a province the oppression of the poor and the violation of justice and right, do not be amazed at the matter; for the high official is watched by a higher, and there are yet higher ones over them.

9 But all things considered, this is an advantage for a land: a king for a plowed field.

10 The lover of money will not be satisfied with money; nor the lover of wealth, with gain. This also is vanity.

11 When goods increase, those who eat them increase; and what gain has their owner but to see them with his eyes?

12 Sweet is the sleep of laborers, whether they eat little or much; but the surfeit of the rich will not let them sleep.

13 There is a grievous ill that I have seen under the sun: riches were kept by their owners to their hurt,

14 and those riches were lost in a bad venture; though they are parents of children, they have nothing in their hands.

15 As they came from their mother's womb, so they shall go again, naked as they came; they shall take nothing for their toil, which they may carry away with their hands.

16 This also is a grievous ill: just as they came, so shall they go; and what gain do they have from toiling for the wind?

17 Besides, all their days they eat in darkness, in much vexation and sickness and resentment.

18 This is what I have seen to be good: it is fitting to eat and drink and find enjoyment in all the toil with which one toils under the sun the few days of the life God gives us; for this is our lot.

19 Likewise all to whom God gives wealth and possessions and whom he enables to enjoy them, and to accept their lot and find enjoyment in their toil—this is the gift of God.

20 For they will scarcely brood over the days of their lives, because God keeps them occupied with the joy of their hearts.

COMMENTS

What would you do if you saw people suffering in poverty and oppression? Would you speak with them to better understand their situation? What would you say to those in powerful positions, those who loved their wealth so much they didn't give a thought to those without? Would you respond by assuring them "you can't take it with you"? Would you simply comment that God gives the wealth, so don't complain"?

The Teacher may be remembering a much older book where the sufferer says: "Naked I came from my mother's womb, and naked shall I return" (Job 1:21; compare a later writer: "For we brought nothing into the world, and we can take nothing out of it," First Timothy 6:7). Job ends up at the same place as The Teacher: there's poverty, disease, injustice, suffering, but the Lord is in charge so it's all good. Here it is stated: "It is our lot." That's just the way it is. People suffer in poverty and oppression but it's supposed to be that way. We all breathe for a short while and then blow away, so don't worry about it, it will soon be over.

The last line is particularly startling, at least for a person with a conscience. The happy, wealthy, secure people ("blessed by God" as some say), don't have to brood over their lives (as The Teacher does) by worrying because they have God's good pleasure, his gifts, and he tops off the cake of contentment with joy in their hearts. These "blessed" people need give no thought to those poor, suffering, oppressed fools who eat in darkness, unseen by the blessed (sound like the preaching of the Prosperity Gospel?).

In the Frank Capra film, "You Can't Take It With You," with Lionel Barrymore, Jean Arthur and Jimmy Stewart, the old wise grandfather tells the rich and foolish businessman: "Maybe it'd stop you trying to be so desperate about making more money than you can ever use? You can't take it with you, Mr. Kirby. So what good is it? As near as I can see, the only thing you can take with you is the love of your friends."

How would The Teacher have written his lecture differently had he good honest friends or an aged grandparent to speak such truth to him?

Playing the playful and quirky grandfather, Barrymore gathers the family around the dinner table and says grace: "Well, Sir, here we are again. We've been getting along pretty good for quite a while now - we're certainly much obliged. Remember all we ask is just to go along the way we are, keep our health; as far as anything else is concerned, we leave that up to you. Thank you."

Nearly the kind of grace Koheleth would say, or might it even be a "secular prayer" to That-Which-Holds-It-All-Together (Nature, Breath)?

Our Teacher could have saved himself some grief by joining in the *Canticle* of Francis of Assisi in praise of

"Brother Sun," "Sister Moon" and "Brother Wind" who praises the Creator/Creation "through the air, cloudy and serene, and every kind of weather." A long, deep breath of gratefulness, in any sacred or secular form, is superior to fearfulness.

NOTES & QUESTIONS

CHAPTER SIX
Breath, Death And Koheleth

Chapter 6: 1-12

1 There is an evil that I have seen under the sun, and it lies heavy upon humankind:

2 those to whom God gives wealth, possessions, and honor, so that they lack nothing of all that they desire, yet God does not enable them to enjoy these things, but a stranger enjoys them. This is vanity; it is a grievous ill.

3 A man may beget a hundred children, and live many years; but however many are the days of his years, if he does not enjoy life's good things, or has no burial, I say that a stillborn child is better off than he.

4 For it comes into vanity and goes into darkness, and in darkness its name is covered;

5 moreover it has not seen the sun or known anything; yet it finds rest rather than he.

6 Even though he should live a thousand years twice over, yet enjoy no good—do not all go to one place?

7 All human toil is for the mouth, yet the appetite is not satisfied.

8 For what advantage have the wise over fools? And what do the poor have who know how to conduct themselves before the living?

9 Better is the sight of the eyes than the wandering of desire; this also is vanity and a chasing after wind.

10 Whatever has come to be has already been named,

and it is known what human beings are, and that they are not able to dispute with those who are stronger.

11 The more words, the more vanity, so how is one the better?

12 For who knows what is good for mortals while they live the few days of their vain life, which they pass like a shadow? For who can tell them what will be after them under the sun?

COMMENTS

A short chapter—short and to the point. But what is the point? Is it sharp or dull? Here again, just as the writer keeps asking that question, so we're invited to ask the same of him. *What's your point?*

If we were reading someone's diary or journal here we might sense we are deeper in their inner sanctum, their hidden world where questions dominate the kingdom within. That may be attractive to some of us, not so much to others. However, flipping through Koheleth as a journal could give us broader insights into his narrower meditations.

Parallels can be found in the *Meditations* of Stoic philosopher and emperor Marcus Aurelius. "Since it is possible that you may leave from life this very moment, make every thought and act count." "The universe is transformation." "Do not act as if you were going to live 10,000 years. Death is present. So while you live, be good." "Live with the gods. Be satisfied with what's been given—a part of Zeus in everyone as a guardian and guide."

The Teacher and the Emperor share a level of agreement: life is brief, keep your words brief, act as if any moment is the last. Where Aurelius could have been a mentor to Koheleth is in emphasizing living well; life may be fleeting but it's never in vain. Stoics were generally not negative about life, just bluntly honest and realistic. "Look within," Marcus teaches, "Within is the fountain of good, and it will always bubble up, if you will only dig." Koheleth asks: "Who knows what is good" or the results or rewards of being good in our short, shadowy lives? And Aurelius replies, in a sense: "Dig within, you'll find good, there's good all around you." This is not a depressing downer philosophy. It only shows the need for more voices along the path of wisdom.

Could we think of "chasing wind" as equivalent to "taking a deep breath"? Holding our breath ... waiting to exhale ... appreciating the in and out cycle through our "windpipe." (Strange as it sounds, I learned to breathe —to be mindful of my breath—by sitting and walking with Zen priests. Yet, breathing is not "spiritual" or religious, but natural).

Facing the wind, inhaling the air, is a life-giving, life-affirming alternative to Bob Seger's "running against the wind." Take a deep breath and keep moving, thinking, seeking understanding. But never ask if the breath is worth drawing into our lungs. In this sense, the wind should indeed be "chased."

Gautama Buddha of India taught: "The scent of flowers does not go against the wind," and: "Just as a fragrant, delightful lotus grows from a heap of dust" so the most enlightened students (and teachers) emerge from those who don't see that they "are like so much dust" (*Dhammapada*, 4:15-16).

NOTES & QUESTIONS

CHAPTER SEVEN
Wise Fools, Foolishly Wise

Chapter 7: 1-14

1 A good name is better than precious ointment, and the day of death, than the day of birth.

2 It is better to go to the house of mourning than to go to the house of feasting;
for this is the end of everyone, and the living will lay it to heart.

3 Sorrow is better than laughter, for by sadness of countenance the heart is made glad.

4 The heart of the wise is in the house of mourning; but the heart of fools is in the house of mirth.

5 It is better to hear the rebuke of the wise than to hear the song of fools.

6 For like the crackling of thorns under a pot, so is the laughter of fools; this also is vanity.

7 Surely oppression makes the wise foolish, and a bribe corrupts the heart.

8 Better is the end of a thing than its beginning; the patient in spirit are better than the proud in spirit.

9 Do not be quick to anger, or anger lodges in the bosom of fools.

10 Do not say, "Why were the former days better than these?" For it is not from wisdom that you ask this.

11 Wisdom is as good as an inheritance, an advantage to those who see the sun.

12 For the protection of wisdom is like the protection of

money, and the advantage of knowledge is that wisdom gives life to the one who possesses it.

13 Consider the work of God; who can make straight what he has made crooked?

14 In the day of prosperity be joyful, and in the day of adversity consider; God has made the one as well as the other, so that mortals may not find out anything that will come after them.

COMMENTS

Turning to popular or "culturally acceptable" sayings, platitudes or cliches, is one way people cope with difficult times or disasters. If Koheleth is indeed Solomon, and if Solomon actually wrote The Proverbs, he is the master of proverbial quips and even jokes. The Teacher apparently saw himself as the Benjamin Franklin of his day. Franklin gave us his own playful proverbs in phrases such as: "What is more valuable than Gold? Diamonds. Than Diamonds? Virtue," "Haste makes Waste," "Search others for their virtues, thy self for thy vices," "It is better to take many injuries than to give one," "Wish not so much to live long as to live well" (*Poor Richard's Almanack*). Some of these lines are deep in our cultural memory, usually thought of with a smile or chuckle. Yet, when mixed with religious beliefs, cultural memory can cause strange, unwise and irrational usages. In our day, someone emerges from the rubble of a disaster, all their neighbors are dead, homes destroyed, and they say: "Thank God! He protected me!" Someone finds a Bible or cross in the ruins of a home or church and says: "It's a miracle!" Some terrible natural or human-caused event happens and politicians fall over themselves to proclaim they are "Sending Thoughts and Prayers!"

How is The Teacher presenting anything different? It would be wise, showing an actual practice of wisdom, to question these neat (or trite) sayings. An aphorism isn't necessarily right or good. It may even sound flippant or foolish. "Better to go to the house of mourning than the house of feasting"? "The day of death is better than the day of birth"? "Better is the end of a thing than its beginning"? Discernment is critical with pop-wisdom, memes, sayings, proverbs and "truisms." Discerning the truth of a "wise thought" may call for deep reflection and more experience. As one popular saying goes, we need to "do a reality-check" on things. And the best freethinker's tool is the "fact-check." What's the reference? Where is the evidence this stuff being passed around, tweeted and posted is true? Wisdom checks things out.

Another interpretation here is that The Teacher is employing a kind of psychological twist to make his point and that point could be to get a rounded education by going places, doing things and thinking "outside the box" (as we say). It's as if he's saying: "Celebration is fine, but attending a funeral sometimes can teach more about life than a party." Or, "Laughing and singing and making light of life is fun, but it can be more instructive sometimes to face sorrow and grief and get a 'reality-check' from a wiser person."

On the other hand, or simply a check and balance, I think of Ben Franklin's excellent witticism: "Hide not your Talents, they for Use were made. What's a Sun-Dial in the shade!" Further confirmation that Koheleth could have learned valuable and worthwhile lessons from Poor Richard.

Then, of course, he falls back on a potentially destructive faith, one content with the attitude that both prosperity and adversity come from God, so consider that, accept that, and realize you may never know why, or what comes later. No one knows the outcome, the consequences, of all our actions. Let it be. And yet, does the writer let it be, let it go, accept life's confounding controversies? It doesn't seem so. He's as lost in the looniness as anyone, and tossing out a string of nice-sounding aphorisms doesn't really help much, does it? Where will he take this next?

Let's eat a little more breath, swallow more wind (maybe take a sip of something) and continue our investigation of a brilliant and bewildered mind.

15 In my vain life I have seen everything; there are righteous people who perish in their righteousness, and there are wicked people who prolong their life in their evildoing.

16 Do not be too righteous, and do not act too wise; why should you destroy yourself?

17 Do not be too wicked, and do not be a fool; why should you die before your time?

18 It is good that you should take hold of the one, without letting go of the other; for the one who fears God shall succeed with both.

19 Wisdom gives strength to the wise more than ten rulers that are in a city.

20 Surely there is no one on earth so righteous as to do good without ever sinning.

21 Do not give heed to everything that people say, or you may hear your servant cursing you;

22 your heart knows that many times you have yourself cursed others.

23 All this I have tested by wisdom; I said, "I will be wise," but it was far from me.

24 That which is, is far off, and deep, very deep; who can find it out?

25 I turned my mind to know and to search out and to seek wisdom and the sum of things, and to know that wickedness is folly and that foolishness is madness.

26 I found more bitter than death the woman who is a trap, whose heart is snares and nets, whose hands are

fetters; one who pleases God escapes her, but the sinner is taken by her.

27 See, this is what I found, says the Teacher, adding one thing to another to find the sum,

28 which my mind has sought repeatedly, but I have not found. One man among a thousand I found, but a woman among all these I have not found.

29 See, this alone I found, that God made human beings straightforward, but they have devised many schemes.

COMMENTS

L isten closely: "In my vain life. . ." By now, we may sense this sums up the entire book fairly well! "I have seen everything," and maybe he has. In his day he might have had unprecedented access to his world, interacting with diverse voices, including his many wives representing distant lands, as we do now with the internet. We've "seen it all," and yet, something new comes across our screens and we wonder again at our ignorance. To "turn the mind," to search, to seek, in the kingdom of Judah or the realm of Google, we may not be that much further on the way of wisdom than The Teacher.

In a description of the beliefs of her Appalachian mountain people, Wilma Dykeman wrote: *"Often comical, occasionally inspiring, the insights into [religious faith] of the people on this mountain river are sometimes simple to the point of absurdity, sometimes profound to the point of wisdom .... As in so much else, here they are a paradox, a sort of symbol of all human wonder and perverseness"* (*The French Broad*, 1955).

Dykeman's mountain folk sound like kin to Koheleth. Comical and insightful, exhibiting both absurdity and wisdom, they are paradox and symbol. "Do not act too wise;" "All this I have tested by wisdom; "I said, 'I will be wise,' but it was far from me." The wise who think they're wise, proud of their wisdom, reveal how much wisdom they lack. More than a timeless Socratic premise, simple, poor, unlearned folk can speak the wisdom we most need to hear and heed. There may be perverseness, irrationality and superstition, but it may be accompanied by wonder and wisdom.

After all, full understanding is far off and very deep, or higher up on a trail he hasn't yet found. There may be ten rulers in a city, hundreds of philosophers and clergy, but wisdom may not reside too much in the metropolis.

English Jesuit poet, Gerard Manley Hopkins, revealed his own kinship with The Teacher when he penned these poetic lines: "O the mind, mind has mountains; cliffs of fall; Frightful, sheer, no-man-fathomed." In his fearful condition he catches the same dark winds of despair: "Wretch, under a comfort serves in a whirlwind: all Life death does end and each day dies with sleep" ("Carrion Comfort," 42).

Koheleth tries to hand over the responsibility for his despair to the entrapment of woman. It's no wonder Elizabeth Cady Stanton, in *The Woman's Bible*, offered incisive critique of The Teacher: "He gave admirable rules for wisdom and virtue ... but failed to practice the lessons which he taught." A harsh evaluation for any instructor. Stanton surmises that the writer "must have had a sad experience in his relations with women" and "his opinion is a grave reflection on his own mother." Quite the Freudian analysis! In fact, Stanton's overall assessment of Ecclesiastes is: "To one whose life has been useful to others and sweet to themselves, it is quite impossible to accept these pessimistic pictures of human destiny."

To our text, there's a frustration and futility when things don't always add up. He's actually trapped in a mathematics of mind, endlessly looking for the sum, the solution, constantly distracted or trapped by someone else to blame—the fools and females—but there's only one thing he discovers in analyzing human behavior: people put up screens and schemes, masks to attract our attention away from facing life truthfully —"straightforward" people are hard to find.

Along with Hopkins, this is his "comfort [served] in a whirlwind." More sucking air, gasping for breath, grasping for meaning.

NOTES & QUESTIONS

CHAPTER EIGHT
Wind Power, Blowin' In The Wind

1 Who is like the wise man? And who knows the interpretation of a thing? Wisdom makes one's face shine, and the hardness of one's countenance is changed.

2 Keep the king's command because of your sacred oath.

3 Do not be terrified; go from his presence, do not delay when the matter is unpleasant, for he does whatever he pleases.

4 For the word of the king is powerful, and who can say to him, "What are you doing?"

5 Whoever obeys a command will meet no harm, and the wise mind will know the time and way.

6 For every matter has its time and way, although the troubles of mortals lie heavy upon them.

7 Indeed, they do not know what is to be, for who can tell them how it will be?

8 No one has power over the wind to restrain the wind, or power over the day of death; there is no discharge from the battle, nor does wickedness deliver those who practice it.

9 All this I observed, applying my mind to all that is done under the sun, while one person exercises authority over another to the other's hurt.

COMMENTS

More unanswerable questions. So he defaults to his royal authority. After all, the king's word is divine, even with his inner doubts and disbelief. Maybe God is like the king, he muses. "He does whatever he pleases" so obey his commands. Except, the nagging reality, the incessant voice in his head whispers: "No one has power over the wind … or the day of death" or anything really. Where lies the greatest power? The wind itself, breath. No wonder centuries of tradition, teachers and preachers have translated the word wind/breath as "spirit." A persistent belief holds: there must be something above, behind, beyond the power of nature; Life has to be more than feeding on wind.

The king, the queen, the teacher, the preacher—these can only command. No one should ask "What are you doing?" yet this is precisely what Koheleth has been doing all along! "What is God doing and why?" The king challenging the King, the teacher questioning the Principal, the preacher doubting higher authorities. Maybe that's it—this is primarily an authority issue. "Who will tell human beings how it will be?" Thankfully he recognizes his own authority and owns the fact that he has the power to exercise that authority "over another to the other's hurt." Is this a not-so-veiled or vain way to question the Higher Authority who appears to exercise power over others, including The Teacher, even when it hurts or harms?

Several classic songs come to mind while reading this chapter. "Blowin' in the Wind" by Bob Dylan, "Both Sides Now" by Joni Mitchell and "Here Comes the Sun" by George Harrison. These may give us wider context for empathizing with the feelings Koheleth expresses. "The answers my friend are blowing in the wind," "I really don't know life, at all," "It seems like years since it's been clear." Though The Teacher laments: "The troubles of mortals lie heavy upon them," as we observe and apply our minds with a wider lens to expand our vision, the fact the sun appears in the sky once again, a new day begins, we might welcome a flicker of hope rising from the darkness, and sing.

The first time he ever heard Quaker reformer Lucretia Mott speak, Frederick Douglass described her as "a glorified presence bearing a message of light ... to a strangely wandering world, straying away from the paths of truth and justice ... where peace is lost and true happiness is sought in vain" ("Honor to Whom Honor"). One imagines Mott and Douglass pulling Koheleth from his high and mighty throne, speaking truth to power, his power, pushing him into the light of radical wisdom where he could truly "apply his mind" to the greater needs of the human community.

Reformers may insist he desist from his moaning to discover "higher purposes," in a sense to command himself, be his own subject. There is a wind of change, wind-power, that is not empty or meaningless, an invisible force sculpting the landscape, re-forming lives in very visible ways.

CHAPTER 8: 10-17

10 Then I saw the wicked buried; they used to go in and out of the holy place, and were praised in the city where they had done such things. This also is vanity.

11 Because sentence against an evil deed is not executed speedily, the human heart is fully set to do evil.

12 Though sinners do evil a hundred times and prolong their lives, yet I know that it will be well with those who fear God, because they stand in fear before him,

13 but it will not be well with the wicked, neither will they prolong their days like a shadow, because they do not stand in fear before God.

14 There is a vanity that takes place on earth, that there are righteous people who are treated according to the conduct of the wicked, and there are wicked people who are treated according to the conduct of the righteous. I said that this also is vanity.

15 So I commend enjoyment, for there is nothing better for people under the sun than to eat, and drink, and enjoy themselves, for this will go with them in their toil through the days of life that God gives them under the sun.

16 When I applied my mind to know wisdom, and to see the business that is done on earth, how one's eyes see sleep neither day nor night,

17 then I saw all the work of God, that no one can find out what is happening under the sun. However much they may toil in seeking, they will not find it out; even

though those who are wise claim to know, they cannot
find it out.

COMMENTS

Death. Deny it or face it. Here again, we can imagine the king in his palace or The Teacher in his ivory tower office gazing down at common people, going about their daily business, birth and wedding celebrations and ... funeral processions. He surmises, none of those people can add a day to their life. Even from high up here I can see that; I can see that no one can see the "big picture."

At this point our musical memories might turn up the volume on Marvin Gaye singing "What's Going On?"

Is the human heart "fully set to do evil"? Is this confirming the doctrine of "original sin"? Hardly. Although ... bad things happen, over and over again, good people suffer, everyone dies and life seems utterly worthless. Some live in a shadow their whole life. Others find light. Fear or revere something higher.

Again The Teacher drops back to his default position: fear Elohim. How do we show that respectful reverence? By doing the best thing we can do—eat, drink, and enjoy ourselves. With all the vanity, all the emptiness and worthlessness, all we can do is fill ourselves with good things (when we can find those or afford those) and get joy any way we can.

He sees "all the work of God" but he really knows nothing about what God is doing. No one can know. He's been clear about that foggy vision. Again, people claim to be wise and know what God is doing (even Koheleth claims that) but they can't explain it, "they cannot find it out."

Wisdom never ceases to shine a light on our innate ignorance. Wisdom is our death. Wisdom is our breath.

Near the conclusion of his powerful work, *Man's Search for Meaning*, psychiatrist Viktor Frankl writes: "The transitoriness of our existence in no way makes it meaningless. But it does constitute our responsibleness." As if to sit Koheleth square in the counseling chair, he continues: "At any moment, [a person] must decide, for better or for worse, what will be the monument of their existence."

Did Koheleth doubt there would be any monument, in stone or scripture, to the fact he had ever breathed one breath? More importantly, did he feel responsibility for the freedom he loved and hated, the privilege he questioned, and even his own troubled mind? His personal search for meaning left him, and leaves us, weighing the balance of our imbalanced existence.

James Baldwin's father was buried on the writer's 19th birthday. The young man was left with contradictory emotions. He knew he would always have to keep two opposites in mind: *Accept the world as it is*, with injustice, death, despair, and *at the same time never accept it.* Baldwin wished his father, whom he struggled with throughout his life, could be present in this tension, "beside me, so that I could have searched his face for the answers which only the future would give me now" (*Notes of a Native Son*).

The Teacher weeps.

NOTES & QUESTIONS

CHAPTER NINE
Dogs, Lions, Fish & Birds

Chapter 9: 1-12

1 All this I laid to heart, examining it all, how the righteous and the wise and their deeds are in the hand of God; whether it is love or hate one does not know. Everything that confronts them

2 is vanity, since the same fate comes to all, to the righteous and the wicked, to the good and the evil, to the clean and the unclean, to those who sacrifice and those who do not sacrifice. As are the good, so are the sinners; those who swear are like those who shun an oath.

3 This is an evil in all that happens under the sun, that the same fate comes to everyone. Moreover, the hearts of all are full of evil; madness is in their hearts while they live, and after that they go to the dead.

4 But whoever is joined with all the living has hope, for a living dog is better than a dead lion.

5 The living know that they will die, but the dead know nothing; they have no more reward, and even the memory of them is lost.

6 Their love and their hate and their envy have already perished; never again will they have any share in all that happens under the sun.

7 Go, eat your bread with enjoyment, and drink your wine with a merry heart; for God has long ago approved what you do.

8 Let your garments always be white; do not let oil be

lacking on your head.

9 Enjoy life with the wife whom you love, all the days of your vain life that are given you under the sun, because that is your portion in life and in your toil at which you toil under the sun.

10 Whatever your hand finds to do, do with your might; for there is no work or thought or knowledge or wisdom in Sheol, to which you are going.

11 Again I saw that under the sun the race is not to the swift, nor the battle to the strong, nor bread to the wise, nor riches to the intelligent, nor favor to the skillful; but time and chance happen to them all.

12 For no one can anticipate the time of disaster. Like fish taken in a cruel net, and like birds caught in a snare, so mortals are snared at a time of calamity, when it suddenly falls upon them.

COMMENTS

The philosophical teacher continues his self-examination and disappointment with the disorder of the world. It may all be "in the hands of Elohim" but little of it makes sense. "The same fate comes to all." Here he assumes again "the hearts of all are full of evil." A deeply depressing thought. Leaves a feeling of hopelessness and helplessness Koheleth is never far from. Being squeezed in a divine hand may not be as desirable as some believe.

But now, somehow, someway, he's feeling that it truly *is* better to be alive than dead. Even a living dog is better than a dead lion.

Of canines and big cats, Henry David Thoreau—a kind of Koheleth in his day— expanded on this line from Ecclesiastes in *Walden*: "A living dog is better than a dead lion. Shall a man go and hang himself because he belongs to the race of pigmies, and not be the biggest pigmy that he can? Let every one mind his own business, and endeavor to be what he was made."

Eat and drink, have fun. Elohim is fine with that. Your delight is his delight. Enjoy your empty and worthless life, do what you do, because that's all you've got and it's all you get (are we feeling encouraged by that?). We're all on our merry way to Sheol (the grave) so leave it all to "time and chance"—if you're a pigmy, be the best and biggest of them all. As racially charged as that appears (keep in mind the Thoreau home was on the Underground Railroad), Thoreau's point is even clearer than Koheleth's: "be all you can be" in the army of humanity, whatever your race, rank, role or religion. Do your best swimming, we never know when we'll be fish caught in a net.

From the palace in Jerusalem and the pond in Concord, the lesson is to "be what we're made" to be. Of course, we have no idea what that is or who we are. Maybe the lion's not really dead?

The formerly enslaved preacher, Sojourner Truth, once stood tall in a angry crowd and said: "It seems that it takes my black face to bring out your black hearts, so it's well I came ... You are afraid of my black face, because it is a looking glass in which you see yourselves" (Nell Painter, *Sojourner Truth: A Life, A Symbol*).

How might this relate to the looking glass in which Koheleth saw love and hate, the wicked and wise, faith or fate?

"Examine it all." Perhaps his wisest words.

13 I have also seen this example of wisdom under the sun, and it seemed great to me.

14 There was a little city with few people in it. A great king came against it and besieged it, building great siege-works against it.

15 Now there was found in it a poor wise man, and he by his wisdom delivered the city. Yet no one remembered that poor man.

16 So I said, "Wisdom is better than might; yet the poor man's wisdom is despised, and his words are not heeded."

17 The quiet words of the wise are more to be heeded than the shouting of a ruler among fools.

18 Wisdom is better than weapons of war, but one bungler destroys much good.

COMMENTS

This short tale seems to stand on its own. Let's call it, "The King's Army vs. the Poor Man's Wisdom." Koheleth lifts up this imaginative story as a great example of wisdom, so we ought to pay attention.

It's fairly straightforward, but we need a clear image: A little village with a small population faces the siege of a great king with a mighty army. Why a king felt the need to attack such a small town seems foolish, even vain. "Now there was found" a villager who was poor yet wise (and maybe he was wise because of his poverty?). Perhaps he had a simple solution, a brilliant plan to defeat the foolish king. Somehow (we don't know how), "by his wisdom" he saves the village. Afterward, no one remembers what he did or who he was.

Koheleth probably made up the story, as a lesson to teach others, and to remind himself of the profound power of wisdom.

The Japanese "Zatoichi" films come to mind. The "blind swordsman" walks from village to village begging for work (he offers massage services). Yet in each town he comes up against ruffians, criminals or overlords who are oppressing or robbing the poor and vulnerable people. Once he steps in to the conflicts, his true skills manifest. His cane conceals a sword. He is a master swordsman who defeats every attacker. Though poor himself, he stands with the powerless. Though blind, he appears to see better than most.

One telling phrase is "The quiet words of the wise." All the shouting, all the lecturing or preaching, all the creeds and scriptures, matter very little when there are calm and quiet words coming from unexpected people and places. Wisdom among the despised, the overlooked, the forgotten.

A timeless story.

NOTES & QUESTIONS

CHAPTER TEN
Flies & Fools, Slaves & Snakes, Falls & Walls

Chapter 10: 1-15

1 Dead flies make the perfumer's ointment give off a foul odor; so a little folly outweighs wisdom and honor.
2 The heart of the wise inclines to the right, but the heart of a fool to the left.
3 Even when fools walk on the road, they lack sense, and show to everyone that they are fools.
4 If the anger of the ruler rises against you, do not leave your post, for calmness will undo great offenses.
5 There is an evil that I have seen under the sun, as great an error as if it proceeded from the ruler:
6 folly is set in many high places, and the rich sit in a low place.
7 I have seen slaves on horseback, and princes walking on foot like slaves.
8 Whoever digs a pit will fall into it; and whoever breaks through a wall will be bitten by a snake.
9 Whoever quarries stones will be hurt by them; and whoever splits logs will be endangered by them.
10 If the iron is blunt, and one does not whet the edge, then more strength must be exerted; but wisdom helps one to succeed.
11 If the snake bites before it is charmed, there is no advantage in a charmer.
12 Words spoken by the wise bring them favor, but the lips of fools consume them.

13 The words of their mouths begin in foolishness, and their talk ends in wicked madness;
14 yet fools talk on and on. No one knows what is to happen, and who can tell anyone what the future holds?
15 The toil of fools wears them out, for they do not even know the way to town.

COMMENTS

More of the poor person's wisdom? Another version of Poor Richard's Almanack? Is The Teacher passing on what he's learned from listening to those who are most often unheard, not listened to or respected for their wisdom? When did that happen? Like the Pope in "The Shoes of the Fisherman," did he sneak out of the palace to mingle with commoners?

We've had dead lions, now dead flies, and snake bites. And fools are always stumbling into the story to fall into pits or get injured on the job. Will The Teacher always compare the wise with the foolish? Does it help when you feel disillusioned, disoriented or disappointed with life to point a finger and say, "See, look, I don't want to be like them"? Could foolishness and folly be in the eye of the beholder? Could wisdom?

His privilege and elitism are on full display here. Slaves on horseback! Princes have to walk! It's a great evil and error to have the foolish (poor?) in positions of power while the (poor) rich folks have to sit in low chairs, even on the floor!

IF some of these reflective remarks are drawn from Koheleth's time down among the common folk, could they be jokes, meant to be humorous, even sarcastic? Even when fools walk along the road everyone can see they are fools. How? Are they poor? Are they eating and drinking and finding joy in their meager lives? Those judged to be fools talk a lot, but as the story of the poor wise villager defeating the mighty army of the king reminded us (are you paying attention Koheleth?), there could be gems of wisdom buried in the babbling of poor fools who may just be the wise in disguise.

The Teacher seems bitten by his own words here. Has he fallen in his own pit? Is he as dull as the axe? Does *he* even know the way to town?

This isn't a matter of "do as I say, not as I do." It's actually, "think about what I say but don't necessarily accept it; do as I do, if you think it's right." We're only hearing him think aloud anyway. How serious would we want someone to take our thoughts in process?

Booker T. Washington spoke forcefully on meaningful toil: "There is as much dignity in tilling a field as in writing a poem [or scripture] ... Nor should we permit our grievances to overshadow our opportunities" (*Atlanta Exposition Address*).

How many opportunities did The Teacher miss by allowing his grief and grievances to overshadow them?

CHAPTER 10: 16-20

16 Alas for you, O land, when your king is a servant, and your princes feast in the morning!

17 Happy are you, O land, when your king is a nobleman, and your princes feast at the proper time—for strength, and not for drunkenness!

18 Through sloth the roof sinks in, and through indolence the house leaks.

19 Feasts are made for laughter; wine gladdens life, and money meets every need.

20 Do not curse the king, even in your thoughts, or curse the rich, even in your bedroom; for a bird of the air may carry your voice, or some winged creature tell the matter.

COMMENTS

Words of a leader who feels their position is threatened, that they've lost respect and others are waiting to take their place. There's something about feasts, parties, corporate dinners, that bring out the best and worst. Is it "noble" to exert one's nobility? Are citizens and subjects happier when they are led by the riches and most elite? Or, as Chinese teacher, Master Kung (Confucius) taught, in the 6th Century B.C.E. a person in leadership should "desire what is good and the people will be good. The character of a ruler is like wind and that of the people is like grass. In whatever direction the wind blows, the grass always bends" (Sayings of Kung, 12:19). The wise teacher of Asia also said: "A person of humanity, wishing to establish their own character, also establishes the character of others, and wishing to be prominent themselves, also helps others to be prominent" (6:28).

This would be another time to imagine how much more balanced, even wise, The Teacher could have been if he enjoyed the company of other teachers in history. If Koheleth shared a glass of wine, or a walk in nature, with Master Kung, Buddha, Jesus, Muhammad (Aristotle, Socrates) and other wisdom teachers, what literature would we have in our hands, what more expansive viewpoints and questions would be available?

How does one speak to the land, to all inhabitants of the realm? When a leader discovers they are really of lower rank, and others are partying, anticipating when their turn comes to rule, a paranoia sets in. What is he afraid of? A plot, a coup of fools?

Beware of committing thought-crimes! One wonders if The Teacher was worried someone may overhear his thoughts, his lecture, his doubtful words. Someone may peek in his journal!

An old saying: "A little bird told me." Not that birds or beasts care what mere humans do on their thrones or phones.

NOTES & QUESTIONS

CHAPTER ELEVEN
Bake & Sow, Then Let It Go

Chapter 11: 1-10

1 Send out your bread upon the waters, for after many days you will get it back.

2 Divide your means seven ways, or even eight, for you do not know what disaster may happen on earth.

3 When clouds are full, they empty rain on the earth; whether a tree falls to the south or to the north, in the place where the tree falls, there it will lie.

4 Whoever observes the wind will not sow; and whoever regards the clouds will not reap.

5 Just as you do not know how the breath comes to the bones in the mother's womb, so you do not know the work of God, who makes everything.

6 In the morning sow your seed, and at evening do not let your hands be idle; for you do not know which will prosper, this or that, or whether both alike will be good.

7 Light is sweet, and it is pleasant for the eyes to see the sun.

8 Even those who live many years should rejoice in them all; yet let them remember that the days of darkness will be many. All that comes is vanity.

9 Rejoice, young man, while you are young, and let your heart cheer you in the days of your youth. Follow the inclination of your heart and the desire of your eyes, but know that for all these things God will bring you into judgment.

10 Banish anxiety from your mind, and put away pain from your body; for youth and the dawn of life are vanity.

COMMENTS

The Teacher overwhelms us—or *under*whelms us—with common sense. It almost seems he's speaking to a child in a nursery. Then we find out he is talking to his young child. Are we insulted, or inspired?

What you send out you'll get back, even if it's soggy and stale bread. Is this commerce or comedy? Spoken in the context of disaster, what is reliable, sustainable? True, where a tree falls, there it will lie, but Koheleth had no comprehension of "nurse logs" and the new growth that creates the next generation of forests. So perceptive in some areas, Koheleth can only speak from his own limited experience. Has he ever sowed a seed or harvested a crop? He seems to be a keen observer of wind but appears ignorant about the breath, that there is no breath in the womb of a mother, especially in the bones of a fetus. At least he admits he doesn't know how anything happens, including birth, death, or how anything is made. He's not entirely sure what will prosper, what will end up being good—a good crop, a good life.

Life may not always be sweet, but light is sweet. Yet, our teacher can't stay with that sweetness. Darkness is coming and a life in darkness is empty.

What does "follow" mean, in practical terms? Followers of various teachers and traditions claim to be following. It is worthwhile to question—to *follow the questions* when it comes to following and followers.

"Follow the inclination of your heart" could be sound advice, but going after "the desire of your eyes" seems strange guidance. A competent parent passes along warning about consequences, but wouldn't tell their child to do whatever they wish, to have no worries even if something causes pain. "God is watching" (the Judge's eyes are on you) is creepy to say the least. "Do what you want but you're being watched" is an odd way of teaching a child responsibility.

Here is another instance where the professorial parent could learn from the Stoic emperor Marcus Aurelius who wrote in his *Meditations*: "Nature is the common parent of all." Healthy parental guidance might emphasize that it's natural to have desires and dreams but be responsible, pay attention to the personal consequences and how your actions are harmful or helpful to others.

NOTES & QUESTIONS

CHAPTER TWELVE
Stardust, Songs & Secrets In The Wind

Chapter 12: 1-8

1 Remember your creator in the days of your youth, before the days of trouble come, and the years draw near when you will say, "I have no pleasure in them";

2 before the sun and the light and the moon and the stars are darkened and the clouds return with the rain;

3 in the day when the guards of the house tremble, and the strong men are bent, and the women who grind cease working because they are few, and those who look through the windows see dimly;

4 when the doors on the street are shut, and the sound of the grinding is low, and one rises up at the sound of a bird, and all the daughters of song are brought low;

5 when one is afraid of heights, and terrors are in the road; the almond tree blossoms, the grasshopper drags itself along and desire fails; because all must go to their eternal home, and the mourners will go about the streets;

6 before the silver cord is snapped, and the golden bowl is broken, and the pitcher is broken at the fountain, and the wheel broken at the cistern,

7 and the dust returns to the earth as it was, and the breath returns to God who gave it.

8 Vanity of vanities, says the Teacher; all is vanity.

COMMENTS

The writer picks up his parental tone. A secular reading of the first verse could be: "Remember your creator," don't forget who made you: your Parents! The sit-down-and-listen intent seems to be: Enjoy youth while you have it, child, because it's going to be a bumpy ride from then on! When we imagine a child hearing these words, and all the words of Koheleth, we might wonder how that felt. Is this good, encouraging advice from a parent, or discouraging and defeating?

The days of trouble are coming. Guards tremble, fears and terrors. Is this a description of judgment day or a coup against the king? Could it be a child's picture-book version of what will happen if the child rejects the parent? Lots of images: sun, moon, stars, birds, trees, grasshoppers all in distress. Cords and bowls and pitchers and wheels. As Dylan sang, "Everything is broken." Some might read into this the result of "original sin," while others may see glimpses of grief and loss, of destruction and death.

But why be concerned? Why stress the distress? If the bowl or the body breaks, the creator, our parent—Life— is near, gave life, receives life.

Make note that throughout his brief lecture, Koheleth never turns to the scriptures of his own community or kingdom. He never cites the authority of clergy. He never mentions prayer or any specific ritual. After all is said and done, and as vain as life is, the reader is compelled to ask: *what is his religion?*

Early American reformer, Frances Wright, said the following in an 1829 lecture on Religion: *"The true Bible is the book of nature, the wisest teacher is the one who most plainly expounds it, the best priest our own conscience, and the most orthodox church a hall of science."* Would this at all describe the religious views of The Teacher? As if speaking directly to Koheleth, Wright said: *"I am content to state to you, my fellow creatures, that all my studies, reading, reflection, and observation, have obtained for me no knowledge beyond the sphere of our planet, our earthly interests, and our earthly duties; and that I more than doubt, whether, should you expend all your time and all your treasure in the search, you will be able to acquire any better information respecting unseen worlds, and future events, than myself."* Can you recall anything Koheleth says about the afterlife, about other worlds, the supernatural? What does he reference most often in his quest for wisdom? The natural world, the human community, his own thoughts.

If Koheleth was our bible, there would be no bible. Koheleth is not scripture. This is not to dismiss the book from the Hebrew canon or set aside references to Elohim in the text. Not at all. This actually recognizes that faith and religion are not central, or essential, to the book or apparently to the life of the writer. Merely mentioning "God" now and then offers the reader nothing substantial and gives no reasonable basis for building a faith position. Wright was right, and so was Koheleth —enjoy life because it's the only one we have and no one knows why things are what they are or what may or may not come later. Mention a deity if you must, but it won't really make any difference. What is, is. A fully secular viewpoint.

Part of a Cherokee hunter's prayer was: "Give me the wind." Which way is the wind blowing? Will an animal pick up my scent? Will the wind work with me and can I cooperate with the wind to be successful? I am a part of the cycle of life, and so is the animal I seek to kill and consume. I will die and be consumed as well. The wind, the breath, is in me, I share that air with all living things, and will one day exhale it back into the currents of wind, breeze and breath.

Dust returns to the earth. That makes sense. Dust to dust; human to humus. The breath returns to the Great Breather of Breath (spirit to Spirit); the drop to the Ocean; the natural to Nature. A touch of Hinduism as well as secularism here. That which has been created cycles back to that which created or caused it. All is absorbed by soil and sky. All goes back where it came from and no one knows where that is. Some say God, Brahman, Elohim, Allah or Heaven. Who knows and what does it matter?

Particles of dust are breathed in every moment, along with minute creatures we share dust with. There is life in dust and dirt. Some things in life *are* vain, but life is not, and vanity alone is not the cleanest air to breathe.

In recent days, Robby Steinhardt, violinist for the 70's Rock band *Kansas* passed away, or blew away, became dust and wind. As you may recall, Kansas was famous for "Dust in the Wind" as well as "Carry On My Wayward Son," both ballads with a strong message perhaps echoing the dirge of The Preacher. "All we are is dust in the wind." Koheleth would no doubt sing along. After all, they're his lyrics.

CHAPTER 12: 9-14

9 Besides being wise, the Teacher also taught the people knowledge, weighing and studying and arranging many proverbs.

10 The Teacher sought to find pleasing words, and he wrote words of truth plainly.

11 The sayings of the wise are like goads, and like nails firmly fixed are the collected sayings that are given by one shepherd.

12 Of anything beyond these, my child, beware. Of making many books there is no end, and much study is a weariness of the flesh.

13 The end of the matter; all has been heard. Fear God, and keep his commandments; for that is the whole duty of everyone.

14 For God will bring every deed into judgment, including every secret thing, whether good or evil.

COMMENTS

Just to complicate matters, now we have another person—his teaching assistant?—stepping in to inform us "what the teacher also taught." The first thing she (why not female?) claims is The Teacher left instructions about knowledge and spoke "words of truth" conveyed through proverbs and sayings. She is the one who has the responsibility for wrapping up the whole seminar, to clean up after the mess we've been handed. Not necessarily a terrible mess, a disorganized and disorienting mess of personal struggles, one person's search for anecdotes he hopes will be antidotes to his despair. Her summary neatly cleans up with a tidy conclusion for the reader: You don't need any other books; it's not necessary to listen to anyone else; just study the wisdom of The Teacher and you'll be fine. Your only homework assignment is to practice what The Professor tried to discover for himself.

Fear God and keep his commandments—that's enough. Is it? How? Begs a bunch of questions: Who is this God and why fear him—is this God worthy of reverence and worship? Which commandments and why should we have to be commanded at all? In later times, another teacher, Jesus of Nazareth, taught that loving God (aka "Love") was the greatest commandment and the second was closely related: to love your neighbor as yourself. Love. Loving Love. Not something Koheleth seemed all that interested in.

Jewish philosopher Martin Buber hinged his perspective of the human condition on the relation of an "I" to a "You" (*I and Thou*). We discover meaning through a meeting of persons. For Buber, both the I and the You were sacred, holy, and in the most "actual" moments it is truly "I-You," a completely reciprocal relation. Then, there is "a drawing of a deep breath during which the You remains present." Heady (and mystical) thought here, but bringing Buber into dialogue with Koheleth might be informative. The Teacher doesn't appear to be in an "I-Thou" relation with the great You (or any You; his son perhaps), but he may feel affinity with Buber's search for the divine: "Whoever goes forth to his You with his whole being and carries to it all the being of the world, finds him whom one cannot seek." Makes the head spin a little, but no more than what The Teacher presents.

We might get a hint at what Buber means if we circle back again and again to *relation*, and embracing a relation with the world that is not an "It" or populated by "Its" but is alive and valuable You. To "find him whom one cannot seek" is an enigmatic way of saying that any "God" worth looking for can't be found as a "God" but only as a relation, a You.

Again, Koheleth might have alleviated at least some of his despair if he could have listened closely to Martin Buber and found the world, and himself, not empty or meaningless but abundantly full of invaluable life. Leaving his tower or temple, he might have experienced "true community" as understood by Buber, a teeming community of people who "stand in a living, reciprocal relationship to a single, living center, and they have to stand in a living, reciprocal relationship to one another." Call that living center "God" if we must, but people must be alive to each other, equal, respected, inclusive, welcoming, sharing in the Life at the center of everything they do, everything they are. This could never be a God of fear. How many gods are alive enough for that?

The Greek philosopher Protagoras reportedly said: "I do not know about the gods ... I have no means of knowing either that they exist or that they do not exist. For many are the obstacles that impede knowledge, both the obscurity of the question and the shortness of human life." The Teacher agrees, to an extent. Then, he takes the leap, back into tradition (tribe, temple, theology), and forward into fate, asking "Who knows?" Well, he says, it's all in the hands of the Great It. He finds no You in the universe or in his life, except in those moments when he resigns himself to the unknown will, unknown purposes of the Unknown divinity.

Why fear the unknown? Why follow the commands of such an inscrutable being who remains elusive behind the scenes and screens?

Are we surprised that "evil" gets the last word, literally? Perhaps the intent is to emphasize the equilibrium, the balance of good and evil? Do they cancel each other out? Or are the final lines of this message closer to what a poet I once knew, who lived under a freeway, said to me one sunny afternoon down in his dark cave of a camp: "The opposite of EVIL is LIVE!" He was emphatic with that last word, stressing that it means to be ALIVE, not simply live. Something to think about, since he was as much a teacher as The Teacher (or any teacher).

We could think more about the "message" presented in this chapter, and the book itself. If the "Sermon on the Mount" was a message on a mountain (any mountain), maybe Koheleth offers, whether we like it or not, a message in the deep valleys, or caves, or under freeways. He speaks to the depressions we stumble into, get stuck or trapped in. Pits of despair, maybe.

The writer leaves an impression of depressions, past, present and future. But does he give us a way out, real hope, or merely leave us down there to figure it out ourselves, to make sense of the senseless and nonsensical, to probe with questions without answers, problems that may have no solutions? I wonder. And I wonder that in the end, when all is said and done, this circles back around to wonder.

Remember the first chapter—the perplexed professor scans the environment, observing the flow of things but not seeing any way of "going with the flow"? We're left with the same dilemma: live with the questions—make them LIVE ... ALIVE—or fall back on the futility of faith, that is, fearful, frail faith. Traditional believers will walk away from The Teacher with more faith, with a more confident assurance God is in control. Like all scripture, it all boils down to God, for Christianists, Jesus. He's the answer, solution and savior for every question or conundrum tossed out by The Teacher, any teacher, any philosopher or scientist or thinker. One might wonder why they don't just toss out the Bible itself, especially Koheleth. Who needs a book when you've got the Lord of the Universe in your pocket (heart, soul)?

Are we only left with fear, with following commands, to find our own way parsing the evil and the good, asking the same questions? After all, is there really, finally, ultimately anything new, different, meaningful, valuable under the sun? Proverbs and platitudes aside, is there nothing left to hold onto, nothing of lasting value? A more startling, secular question is: Does there need to be?

Koheleth's secrets have been handed to us. We hold in our hands what he has said, and what he has not said. As we blow off the dust of the centuries, we inhale some. Can we judge? Are some of his secrets our secrets too?

NOTES & QUESTIONS

CONCLUDING REFLECTIONS

Wisdom Between The Lines

(or, What's the Use of Ecclesiastes?)

We close the book, put it down, get something to eat and drink, and wonder: have we found joy? A weary, worn-out and perhaps burned-out teacher/preacher/king has left a heavy question hanging from the branches of our brains: What remains worthy in a seemingly worthless life?

Has he left us one of the greatest correctives to the certainties of orthodox religion and religious supremacy? The vanity of so much religious belief and privilege still requires confrontation. The more we accumulate things, including cherished beliefs, the more we become attached to protecting them, defending the thick walls of theology. It's a hard lesson to learn: the more we store *up* and save *up*, the more we'll lose, the more empty—*down in the dumps* and *down and out*—we feel. It's a no brainer but takes a brain to figure it out: there is no way to figure out what it all means, what it's all worth, if anything. So accept the uncertainties. Whine a little with your wine, if it helps (Koheleth did).

In her book, *Doubt: A History,* Jennifer Michael Hecht respects The Teacher/Philosopher and his "wildly surprising message." In summarizing the historical impact of the man and his message, she asserts: "Koheleth was a premier figure in the history of doubt. He was rationalist, while maintaining a bright sense of paradox and mystery; he suggested behaviors and meditations to learn to bear a seemingly harsh reality [and] his book became part of one of the most famous cultural works of humankind."

Like any instructor whose course is worth taking, like any preacher whose sermons are worth hearing, Koheleth encourages curiosity, active skepticism, open investigation, a capacity and commitment to critical free-thinking. In the chaotic classroom of Koheleth, ripe questions hang down low or fall like leaves: What is life? What should I do? What work is needed? If there is a God, what's God up to? What good is it to gain the world and lose your sanity? (a Teacher in Nazareth picks up this theme centuries later, poking fun at Koheleth/Solomon: "Take a look at the flowers, they don't work or worry, yet get this, even old Sol with all his wealth and wisdom wasn't as fashionable as these plants"—Luke 12).

There is another takeaway from the lecture we've read, a more humanistic, naturalistic interpretation--an outlook on life, the world, and our place in the world, that accepts this is the only world we know and quite likely the only world there is. Without any knowledge or guarantee of another existence somewhere, we are left to discover and discern what is best and where to go from here. Koheleth is one of our secular teachers too. Yes, he refers and defers to his tribe's Elohim, but essentially teaches it's up to us, to do what we determine is "given" for us to do—that is, what alternatives are presented to us to choose from in life—and do the best we can. "Do the best you can" may be one of the most fundamental homework assignments to take away from Koheleth's lecture.

In this sense we could say Koheleth hands us some of the most timely wisdom teachings for our day. This may irritate some in the secular community (primarily agitated, anti-religious atheists, for whom the Bible is all vanity anyway) but I think it's reasonable. This may be particularly true since *Koheleth also writes more questions in large letters on the whiteboard of religion:* What is the value of religion? Does religious faith really help, face to face with the great questions of life? How does faith assist with honest doubt, depression and personal disappointments? Faithful freethinkers as well as secular freethinkers need have no fear addressing these difficult questions. In fact, when we ask them together, respecting our common uncertainties, we may stumble into some solutions, however tentative and tenuous.

An Episcopal priest summarizes Ecclesiastes in unsurprising terms: *"No matter how wise or rich or successful one may be, one cannot find meaning in life apart from God. In Ecclesiastes, the fact that "all is vanity" should drive all to fear God, whose work endures forever ... Ecclesiastes describes the meaninglessness of living without God."* As with most conservative Christian approaches to this book, he carries out exactly what he carried in, finding yet another affirmation that faith, his faith, is solid and "biblical." Another evangelical website states the book is: "one of the few books of the Old Testament that the early church debated not including in the Bible."

This preacher also claims the purpose of the book is to present the meaninglessness of life, that, *"answers to the hard questions of life are not forthcoming. On these terms the book confronts the crookedness and uncertainty of life and shows, probably unconsciously, the need for a concept of resurrection to bring harmony out of the discord of reality. The message of Ecclesiastes is that the course of life to be pursued is a God-centered life. The pleasures of life are not intrinsically fulfilling and cannot offer lasting satisfaction, but they can be enjoyed as gifts from God."* The confident bible teacher concludes with this cringe-worthy proclamation: "We should accept what God sends our way, whether blessings or adversity." Would people suffering in poverty, pain or powerlessness find this to be "good news"? Would Koheleth himself embrace that view? Is this truly the summation of biblical theology and religion?

In biblical studies we learn to do "exegesis" (literally to "lead out" the meaning of the text) and we are warned away from "eisegesis" (literally to "lead into" the text). As I see it, most of the time with holy books the most honest admission would be we all "lead into" the text. We bring a lot of baggage—upbringing, culture, education, religious literacy (or not). Our own biases and ignorance. This is the main reason the subtitle of this book is an important caveat: "A Secular Reading." Not "the" secular reading, but one, mine; I'm bringing my biases and life experience, my points of view, into the text. That's just honest. What if every preacher or teacher of the Preacher or Teacher in Ecclesiastes was that straightforward, admitting their exegesis is grounded and guided in their personal eisegesis? I could respect that.

For some who still think of the Hebrew Bible as the "Old Testament" (that old Jewish book) and feel that Christianism is superior to Judaism and all other "isms" (religious supremacy in a Christianist frame), Ecclesiastes will probably always be about the ecclesia, their sectarian ecclesia (*ecclesia*: church). For those of us who emerged from that mindset, it's nearly impossible to nudge someone away from the eisegesis in the head that "it's all about Jesus"—everything in the "old" parts of the scriptures point to the coming of the One who will rescue the Jews, save the Preacher from hell, and make everyone Christian. Getting liberated from that —an eisegetical exit from restrictive faith—is such a relief. *On the other side of faith (speaking personally now), to eat, drink and find joy in life isn't vain or meaningless.* The focus is not on self-salvation, converting the world to my point of view, or spending eternity with the Great Royal Self in another world. Humanist ethics are centered on the inter-connected, interdependent nature of human life, that people should "find joy" for themselves but not in isolation, concerned for the fulfillment of others as well.

A humanist reading of a book like Ecclesiastes is a challenge. I discovered this while reading it again after many years. Now that I've grown quite allergic to theology, I had to consistently ask myself: Am

I "bracketing" the theological, skimming over the references to God? In some sense, yes, of course I was. But each time I considered the theistic framework the Teacher retreats to when confused and depressed, I tried to see with my chaplain's eye, I asked the most humanist of questions: What inner suffering, what personal pain, led him to that belief? Detecting unhealthy tendencies in his beliefs, I had to ask: What kind of God is he turning to for refuge, and is that a rational refuge? At times this deity appears to be very manipulative, arbitrary and pleased to be the Judge of good and evil— in other words, to render judgment on humanity ... the humanity this God created, this creator who destroys as well, who gives good things to some but not to others, who makes some rich and some poor, who makes kings either wise or foolish, who set us up on the earth to live in the midst of injustice, uncertainty and worthlessness--in sum, a deity who can't seem to take a breath as deep as deep space and admit they aren't "doing the best they can."

While we're chasing our next breath, this god seems to sit calmly in the eye of the hurricane of humanness s/he created.

Is there nothing new under the sun when it comes to religion, faith, scriptures? Sometimes I wonder. We seem stuck in the loop, offering the same tired solutions before the problems are identified, preaching the same old gospel that isn't new, good OR news, really. Not for us. Not now. As I often say, the "new" testament is now very "old," so what's next? And what of the totality of

the world's religious traditions? So old; so male dom-
inated; so distracted by rote ritual, theology and traditional thinking.

What's next for religious faith? How much is worthless,
how much vain? Ecclesiastes may offer something radically new—really new. Yes, it will seem to be very old,
but if applied, quite fresh, innovative, inclusive. The
Teacher exposes our deepest questions, fears, hopes and
wisdom not only for ourselves but for the next gener-
ations. Proverbial aphorisms sound nice, make us smile
or think, but ultimately offer little to assist the trap--the
dilemma--of being human.

Another major lesson we can't overlook concerns *power*.
Koheleth struggles with this because he held so much
power, and though he may not have succeeded in learning or living his own wise discoveries, we can. He
presents us with a perpetual puzzle: You can have
great power, privilege, personal wealth and possessions,
plus the best education money can buy—and still be
ignorant, foolish, doubtful and depressed. Should we
be sympathetic to this pathetic predicament of those
who seem to "have it all." Those among the rich and
powerful whose massive egos match their massive for-
tunes can't buy our admiration or respect, but they can
potentially serve, like The Teacher, to instruct us in
what *not* to do, what *not* to seek. It may be one of the
wisest techniques of a good teacher to point to themselves: "See what I have, what I've become; you don't
want to follow this path; there are better, wiser ways to
be 'wealthy' beyond power and possessions. Knowledge

is great. Pleasure is nice, for a time. But life is more. And don't ask me how to discover *the more* of your own life."

No wonder in the Hebrew Bible, the *Book of Lamentations* follows Ecclesiastes! Who wouldn't feel like lamenting after Koheleth/Solomon spills his guts! In some sense it's similar to being with someone who's just had a "meltdown," an episode or attack of some kind —physical or mental. They "act out" or, as we used to say with a degree of respectful humor, an individual is exhibiting "trauma drama" or being a "psychic tornado." You won't understand that unless you've been there, until you have suffered with the suffering, when someone can become "insufferable." Mental illness is no joke, and neither is severe depression. I have plenty of personal experience with that. Yet this raises a not insignificant point: If the writer of Koheleth could laugh at himself, could take himself less seriously, and find humor—even dark humor—in his life and world, maybe he would have found a way through. In fact, without the added words from his "teaching assistant,"—or the fact that the book, or lecture, needed to be completed by someone else—we might wonder if The Professor committed suicide at the conclusion! Intellectual capacity, great knowledge and an active pursuit of wisdom don't guarantee happiness or mental stability. Neither does religious faith.

Ecclesiastes is not for the faint of heart or the frail of mind. It's tough truth if not tough love, beginning in dire uncertainty and ending in fear, if only fear of a rather unjust deity who may be having his own "trauma drama" causing psychic tornadoes then and now.

How to draw conclusions from a book, a lecture, a scripture, that offers no clear conclusions! "Eat, drink and find joy" isn't a conclusion, it's a motivational message to keep seeking, searching, questioning and journeying toward whatever we might find beyond books and teachers, perhaps beyond religion itself.

Koheleth/Ecclesiastes/Teacher/Preacher should be essential reading, a required course, for our time, any time, all seasons. For everything there is indeed a season, yet no one can tell us what season of life we are in, or how to give and get the most of it. As any competent philosopher, Koheleth hands us answers to life and each answer is a question, but also a quest, an invitation to an adventurous interrogation of each of life's circumstances—probing the circumference of our world to make sense of it if we can, and let the uncertainties pass like the clouds. Not to deny the weather patterns of living, but to somehow be ok with a precarious peace, as unstable as that feels. *This is not a resignation to what has been, or is now in the present, but a contemplation of what could be*, that eternal flow that can be as destructive as a hurricane or restorative as our next breath.

When I was an evangelical youth, and even through college and seminary, I kept stored in my mind the old truism: "Your life may be the only Bible anyone ever reads." Extrapolating from that wise (though limited) saying, let's imagine Koheleth is the only biblical book someone ever reads. Apart from the stories of Abraham and Sarah, Moses, the kings and prophets, Jesus, the apostles and Paul, does the message of The Teacher present a summary, a proclamation of the whole? And what of *all* scriptures, all holy books of the world—imagine if Koheleth was the only one. Surely all wisdom can't be contained in this one old book of twelve short chapters and there's no arguing it lacks a dramatic storyline, epic narratives and extensive theology. Yet, that may be one of the greatest strengths of the twelve-chapter treatise, when we creatively imagine The Teacher's lecture as a kind of "last lecture," not as revealed truth but as a raw reality-check on education itself, on religion, even on political power and psychological analysis, perhaps it gives us enough to work with. This is imaginative, but what if? I'm only suggesting the reader entertain the thought, since "what ifs" are part and parcel of the text we are handling.

The first philosophy text I read in college, Will Durant's *The Story of Philosophy*, opens with the words: "There is a pleasure in philosophy … ." I wasn't so sure this "heavy" subject was worth the mental effort, but if it could be a pleasure, I was game. As intimidating as philosophy first appeared to my young evangelical mind, I was intrigued, then hooked, then chose to major in the discipline! In significant ways, philosophy was my bridge out of dogmatic thinking. So many great minds, so many questions and investigations into matters that troubled me as it did them: What is true, good, right, beautiful, valuable? What makes life worth living? On the first page of his introduction, Durant gave me a long-lasting quote from the pond philosopher of *Walden*, Henry Thoreau: *"To be a philosopher is not merely to have subtle thoughts, nor even to found a school, but so to love wisdom as to live, according to its dictates, a life of simplicity, independence, magnanimity and trust."* With each independent thinker I met along the way, I kept in mind, as I do today, the pleasure of loving wisdom, and those four qualities of life remain foundational.

Koheleth, the kingly philosopher (or royal pain in the backside?), had his moments of philosophical pleasure as well, though at times he seems as reticent as that young evangelical student facing the first principles of wisdom. The challenge of a "love of wisdom" is that the love must be practiced, embodied, exercised beyond the mind. And the philosophical endeavor as a practice is a lifelong search with few conclusions to set in concrete and sit on. The Teacher, apparently without the benefit of good and wise mentors, assumes *the usefulness of wisdom is to point out the uselessness of life* (including work and knowledge itself). What he could have learned from Thoreau and many other practitioners of the way of wisdom is that it is indeed a way, a path, a journey, an adventure, a neverending process that assumes progress—that learning is good and meaningful, as is much of life. Koheleth resisted that process, perhaps never quite gaining the wisdom necessary to seek out a useful life beyond empty thinking, to discover how to be useful himself. One great lesson from this book is it takes courage (or for some, faith) to push forward with a practical philosophy consistently searching for what is useful knowledge and useful living.

And usefulness comes into sharper focus when confronting mortality. If we spend our lives questioning our usefulness, interrogating the worth, value or goodness of life, we lose the time. Death can be the *greatest distraction* from life and living. At the same time, literally in the same moments of deepest contemplation, the thought and reality of death can be the *greatest liberation*, to live better, more fully, more consciously. Koheleth may or may not have missed this liberation. That remains an open mystery.

In her poem, "Prophecy," Black feminist priest Pauli Murray expresses her vision of a "new American": "I am the child of kings and serfs, freemen and slaves, Having neither superiors nor inferiors, Progeny of all colors, all cultures, all systems, all beliefs. I have been enslaved, yet my spirit is unbound." She ends the poem with these powerful lines: "I seek no conquest, no wealth, no power, no revenge; I seek only discovery, of the illimitable heights and depths of my own being" (*Dark Testament*). Does it need restatement? Koheleth needed Pauli Murray too. More life, wider experience, on the street listening—escape from the castle, classroom and cathedral (temple, faith, religion).

The Teacher's lecture might leave us, his students, in dark dissatisfaction, but we don't need to stay in that ditch of depression. We have the power to climb out into the light (reason, understanding, perspective), because indeed we live and move and have our being "under the sun." We may fear or revere a supreme being who has it all under control, who demands and commands obedience, or we may fearlessly face the wonderfully uncontrollable nature of human life with humility and resilience. Nevertheless, The Teacher is correct: We're in this thing called Life on Earth together, and in the grand scheme of the Creative Breath (or Evolution) there is always and forever potent potential, endless opportunities to explore open landscapes with open eyes and open minds.

I have a degree of agreement with Philip Novak's assessment of Koheleth's "skepticism and pessimism" (*The World's Wisdom*). I'm not so sure I fully accept his view that: "Conspicuously absent are a sense of humanity's high moral calling," though I understand he is placing Ecclesiastes in the "reconciliation" theme of most biblical literature. I think The Teacher is very much interested in reconciling wind with Wind, breath with Breath, humans with Humanity, or, from a faith perspective, the creature with Creator. The problem or issue is: how, and to what purpose?

For a time, for a season, we might surmise, Koheleth couldn't see beyond his own myopic vision, his self-absorbed despair standing naked before the apparent worthlessness of Life. With our hindsight we can see he was only watching one channel: Vanity Vision, or gazing into a smudged looking glass.

Gratefully, in our time, we can change the channel, turn

off the screens and turn back to this book in any season of life, if it can help us become better human beings. After millenia we may still find worth and wisdom in the teachings themselves, even in what he left out or, as Rabbi Levi Yitzak said, in the white space between the letters and words. Philosopher William James said for something to be "true" it must have "cash value"--it must be pragmatic, useful for our lives. This remains the test, not only for the students but for the teacher known as Ecclesiastes.

Dusty as we are, we take a deeper breath, feel more alive, and stand beside those who are out of breath, who may feel like the deflated Teacher. Getting our "second wind," our "toil" can be energized by a radical hope that others may eat, drink and find joy without having to chase after clean air to breathe or reasonable things to believe. Guided by humility and humanistic ethics, we may listen to Koheleth as one teacher among many, whose wise voice directs each generation toward a more secular future under the sun.

NOTES & QUESTIONS

ABOUT THE AUTHOR

Chris Highland was born and raised near Seattle, then lived in the San Francisco Bay Area for over three decades. He has degrees from Seattle Pacific University and San Francisco Theological Seminary. He was an interfaith chaplain and Presbyterian minister for many years. He has been a special education instructor in a private school and the director of a county emergency shelter. For six years he was the manager of two cooperative homes for independent seniors.

Chris has taught courses in congregations and been an instructor at Dominican University of California, Cherry Hill Seminary, College of Marin and Blue Ridge Community College. He currently teaches courses on Freethought at the Reuter Center on the campus of the University of North Carolina, Asheville. He writes the weekly "Highland Views" column for the *Asheville Citizen-Times*.

His numerous books include:
From Faith to Freethought
Friendly Freethinker
Broken Bridges
A Freethinker's Gospel
Simply Secular
Nature is Enough
Birds, Beetles, Bears and Beliefs
Was Jesus a Humanist?
A Secular Gospel

The Message on the Mountain
Meditations of John Muir
My Address is a River
Jesus and John Muir

Chris is married to Carol Hovis, a Presbyterian minister and spiritual director. They live in the Blue Ridge Mountains in Asheville, North Carolina.

For more information:

Friendly Freethinker (www.chighland.com)

To contact Chris:

chris.highland@gmail.com

"Of making many books there is no end. . ."

~Koheleth 12:12

9 798466 609332